It's the circumstances

A psychologist's contrarian guide to depression, systems, and why your brain might be fine

Psychology that helps you

Lee Hopkins

Claude LeClerque

°138

This book is intended for informational purposes only and should not be used as a substitute for professional medical advice, diagnosis, or treatment. The information contained herein is not meant to be used to make medical decisions or as a basis for self-diagnosis or self-treatment.

Readers are strongly advised to consult with a qualified healthcare professional, preferably a psychiatrist or clinical psychologist, before making any health-related decisions or taking any action based on the content of this book. The author and publisher disclaim any liability for any adverse effects resulting directly or indirectly from the use of or reliance on information contained in this book.

Published by degrees138, Adelaide, South Australia—degrees138.com

For my mother, who always wanted to be able to tell her friends, "my son is a doctor."

I would have been a terrible doctor, mum; people would have died.

“Any idiot can face a crisis; it's this day-to-day living that wears you out.”

— Anton Chekhov

“Human beings are so made that the ones who do the crushing feel nothing; it is the person crushed who feels what is happening. Unless one has placed oneself on the side of the oppressed, to feel with them, one cannot understand.”

— Simone Weill

"The development of higher psychological functions is a product of the social environment."

— Lev Vygotsky

Acknowledgments

This book wouldn't exist without the veterans I've worked with over the years—the ones who trusted me with their stories whilst I was still figuring out my own. You taught me that depression is often a reasonable response to circumstances that would make anyone struggle, and that resilience is what we demand when we refuse to provide actual support. I hope I've done justice to what you shared.

To my fellow neurodivergent humans who've survived decades of masking whilst being told you're fine, actually, you just need to try harder: I see you. The exhaustion is real. The systems are badly designed. You're not broken.

Gaye Idec, my Brisbane-based colleague and friend, read early drafts with the kind of rigorous compassion that only comes from someone who actually understands systemic problems whilst working within imperfect systems trying to help real people. Your feedback made this book better, and your friendship has made life more bearable through some extraordinarily difficult years. Thank you for not telling me to think more positively about circumstances that were objectively crushing me.

To the researchers whose work informed this book—particularly Joanna Moncrieff, Michael Marmot, Kate Pickett and Richard Wilkinson, and countless others who've asked uncomfortable questions about why wealthy countries have such high depression rates—thank you for doing the rigorous work that makes books like this possible. I've tried to cite you properly and not misrepresent your findings, though any errors in interpretation are entirely mine.

To the expat community in Đà Lạt who've created a space where broken people accidentally fix themselves through better circumstances and mutual understanding: you've demonstrated that community support works better than individual resilience, and that different environments produce different outcomes even with the same brains. Cảm ơn nhiều.

I need to acknowledge something unusual: this book was written in collaboration with Claude, an AI system created by Anthropic. Not because I couldn't write it myself—the ideas, experiences, research, and arguments are all mine—but because sometimes you need a conversational partner who can help shape sprawling thoughts into coherent chapters whilst maintaining your voice rather than imposing their own. Claude served as writing tool, sounding board, and occasionally as a mirror reflecting back when I was slipping into academic earnestness instead of conversational warmth. The technology is strange and new and raises questions about authorship we're still figuring out as a society, but transparency seemed more important than pretending I wrote every word in isolation. The lived experience and hard-won insights are mine; Claude helped me articulate them more clearly than I might have managed whilst still depressed in Australia.

To anyone reading this who's currently trapped in crushing circumstances: your response is probably reasonable even if everyone's telling you it's not. I don't have solutions, just observations that circumstances matter enormously and systems could be different if we decided to make them different. That might not be sufficient, but it's what I've got.

Finally, to the universe that spent billions of years evolving consciousness and then apparently decided depression was a reasonable feature to include: your sense of humour is noted and not entirely appreciated, but I'm still here despite your best efforts. Thanks for that, I suppose.

Definitions

Terms that might need explaining (or: The bit where I define things without being patronising)

Look, I've tried to write this book for intelligent mid-teens onwards, which means I've assumed you can follow along without needing everything explained like you're five. But there are some terms that come up repeatedly—some from psychology, some from my research, some from Australian culture—that might be unfamiliar. So here's a quick guide.

I've kept it conversational because if I wanted to write like a textbook, I'd have written a textbook. And nobody needs that.

The psychology and neuroscience bits

Chemical imbalance theory The idea that depression is caused by low levels of serotonin (or other neurotransmitters) in your brain. This has been the dominant explanation for depression for about forty years and is used to justify prescribing antidepressants to millions of people. Small problem: the research evidence doesn't actually support it.

Which is awkward for everyone who's built careers and profits on this theory, but there you go.

SSRIs and SNRIs Selective Serotonin Reuptake Inhibitors and Serotonin-Norepinephrine Reuptake Inhibitors. Antidepressants that supposedly work by increasing serotonin (or serotonin and norepinephrine) in your brain. They do help some people—I'm not anti-medication—but we're less certain about *why* they help than pharmaceutical companies would have you believe.

Cognitive Behavioral Therapy (CBT) A type of therapy that focuses on identifying and challenging "negative thought patterns." The idea is that if you think differently, you'll feel differently. Works brilliantly when your thoughts are actually distorted. Less brilliantly when your thoughts are accurate assessments of genuinely difficult circumstances. Hard to challenge "I can't afford rent" with cognitive techniques when your bank statement keeps agreeing with you.

Psychological contract The unwritten, implicit expectations between two parties—originally used in organisational psychology to describe employer-employee relationships, but applicable to any relationship where there are unspoken promises. I worked hard, you provide security. I serve my country, you take care of me. When these unspoken promises are violated, people experience profound distress. My research area for decades, and yes, I will bang on about it.

Person-environment fit Exactly what it sounds like: how well a person's characteristics align with their environment's demands. High fit = thriving. Low fit = constant friction. Like wearing shoes that don't quite fit—not unbearable, but you're always aware of the discomfort.

The neurodivergence bits

Neurodivergent and neurotypical Neurodivergent means your brain works differently from what society considers "standard" or "typical." Includes autism, ADHD, dyslexia, and other conditions. Neurotypical means your brain works in the way society has designed systems around. Not better or worse—just different. Like Macs versus PCs, except with more social consequences.

Autism (or Autism Spectrum Disorder) A neurological difference affecting how people communicate, process sensory information, and interact socially. Not a disease. Not something requiring cure. Just a different neurological operating system. Comes in wide variety—hence "spectrum." Some autistic people need significant support; others (like me) learn to mask well enough to pass as neurotypical whilst being exhausted by the effort.

ADHD (Attention Deficit Hyperactivity Disorder) Another neurological difference affecting attention, impulse control, and executive function. Despite the name, it's not really about deficit—more about attention being interest-driven rather than priority-driven. Can hyperfocus intensely on interesting things whilst struggling to focus on boring-but-necessary things. Also not a disease. Also exhausting to manage in systems designed for neurotypical brains.

AuDHD Autism and ADHD occurring together. Apparently makes me a limited-edition collector's item in the neurodivergent community. Creates interesting combination where some traits amplify each other (social exhaustion + need for routine meets need for novelty + impulsivity = interesting times).

Masking (or camouflaging) The process of hiding your autistic or ADHD traits to appear neurotypical. Monitoring every word and gesture, following scripts for social situations, suppressing stims, forcing eye contact. It's not conscious deception—it's survival strategy learned young. And it's absolutely exhausting. Like running a marathon whilst everyone else is walking to the shops, but because you're keeping up, they assume you're also walking.

Executive function Brain functions involving planning, organisation, time management, initiating tasks, switching between tasks. ADHD brains often struggle with executive function, which is why I might research quantum physics for six hours but forget to eat or can't make myself respond to important emails. Not laziness. Different wiring.

Stimming Self-stimulatory behaviour. Repetitive movements or sounds that help regulate sensory input and emotional state. Hand-flapping, rocking, humming, fidgeting. Autistic and ADHD people often stim naturally, then learn to suppress it because it's considered "weird." Suppressing stims takes energy. More masking exhaustion.

The systemic and political bits

Systemic versus individual Systemic = problems arising from how systems are designed. Individual = problems arising from personal characteristics or choices. Depression being treated as individual problem (your brain is broken) versus systemic problem (systems are crushing people). Most mental health treatment focuses on individual interventions whilst ignoring systemic causes.

Universal Basic Income (UBI) Regular payment to all citizens regardless of employment status, with no conditions attached. Not welfare—everyone gets it, rich or poor. Research shows it doesn't make people lazy; it reduces poverty, improves mental health, and lets people make better long-term decisions. Politically controversial because it requires trusting people and costs money that currently goes elsewhere.

Means-testing Proving you're poor enough to deserve government support. Involves providing bank statements, asset declarations, repeated verification that you haven't hidden resources. Creates poverty trap because having any savings disqualifies you. Also creates constant surveillance and degradation. Costs more to administer than it saves in prevented fraud, but we do it anyway.

Social determinants of health The circumstances in which people are born, grow, live, work, and age. Things like poverty, education, employment, housing, discrimination, social connections. Research shows these determine health outcomes more than individual biology or healthcare access. But healthcare systems prefer treating individual symptoms to addressing social determinants because the latter requires systemic change.

Resilience (as used in mental health) Supposed positive quality of bouncing back from adversity. Sounds good until you realise it's often used to celebrate people surviving circumstances that shouldn't exist whilst avoiding fixing those circumstances. "Look how resilient they are!" versus "Why are we creating circumstances that require superhuman resilience to survive?" I'm suspicious of resilience as concept because it individualises systemic problems.

The Australian culture bits

Tall poppy syndrome Australian cultural tendency to cut down anyone who gets too successful or acts like they're better than others. Rooted in egalitarian values—nobody should think they're special. In practice, means you can't be too successful, too smart, or too different without people resenting you. Makes self-promotion feel culturally transgressive, which is problematic if you're trying to run a business.

"She'll be right" Australian phrase meaning "don't worry, it'll be fine, no point stressing." Meant to be reassuring. Often used to dismiss genuine problems without addressing them. Particularly brutal when combined with cultural prohibition against admitting you're not fine. Your house is falling apart? She'll be right. Can't afford food? She'll be right. Suicidal? She'll be right mate, have a beer.

Mateship Australian ideal of friendship and mutual support. Mates look after mates. Sounds lovely in theory. In practice, has rules about what support is acceptable. Can rely on mates for practical help (moving furniture, borrowing tools) but not emotional support without making it weird. Real blokes don't have feelings requiring discussion, apparently.

Centrelink Australian government agency administering welfare payments and benefits. Technically Services Australia now, but everyone still calls it Centrelink. Known for: phone queues lasting hours, arbitrary payment suspensions, Byzantine bureaucracy, treating recipients as potential fraudsters requiring constant surveillance. Source of much despair.

DVA (Department of Veterans' Affairs) Australian government department supposedly supporting veterans. In practice, provides pensions below poverty line whilst making you prove repeatedly that you actually served. Has excellent customer service charter promising respect and efficiency. Reality somewhat different.

The general concepts that might need clarifying

Gaslighting Psychological manipulation making someone question their own perception of reality. Named after 1938 play *Gas Light* where husband manipulates wife into thinking she's insane. Systems gaslight people by reframing contract violations as individual failures. You were promised security if you worked hard, didn't get it, and now you're told you didn't work hard enough rather than acknowledging the promise was broken.

Cognitive load Amount of mental processing capacity being used. Poverty creates high cognitive load because you're constantly calculating, planning, worrying. Uses up mental resources that could otherwise be devoted to other things. Research shows poverty reduces cognitive function by equivalent of 13 IQ points just from this load.

Circumstantial versus biological depression My distinction, not official diagnostic categories. Circumstantial depression = reasonable response to unreasonable circumstances. Biological depression = genuine neurological condition requiring treatment regardless of circumstances. Most depression is probably mix of both, but we treat everything as primarily biological whilst ignoring circumstances.

There. Terms explained without excessive handholding or dumbing down. You're welcome to skip this section entirely if you worked everything out from context, which you probably did because you're not thick.

If there's anything else that's unclear, that's on me for not explaining it properly in the main text. Though I suspect most confusion will come from questioning whether I'm serious about things I'm absolutely serious about, or questioning whether I'm joking about things I'm absolutely joking about.

Welcome to my communication style. It's like this all the way through.

Contents

Foreword

I've known Lee Hopkins for three years, and I've watched him ask uncomfortable questions that most psychologists prefer to avoid. This book is full of those questions, and they matter more than we'd like to admit.

We've built an entire industry around helping individuals cope with circumstances that shouldn't exist in the first place. We medicate reasonable responses to unreasonable situations. We teach resilience to people surviving systems that are actively hostile to human flourishing. We celebrate those who escape whilst ignoring the millions who remain trapped.

And we call this mental healthcare.

Lee's argument is deceptively simple: what if depression is often a sane response to insane circumstances? What if we're treating symptoms whilst carefully ignoring causes? What if the problem isn't broken brains but broken systems?

These aren't new questions—critical psychologists have been asking them for decades. But Lee brings something most critics lack: he's lived it. He's experienced the crushing weight of systems designed to help but structured to harm. He's navigated poverty whilst owning property, survived on a military pension below the poverty line, spent sixteen hours on hold with Centrelink, and ultimately fled the country to survive.

His depression lifted not through better medication or more therapy or increased resilience, but through environmental change. Same brain, different circumstances, completely different outcomes.

That should concern us.

If a trained psychologist with decades of experience, academic credentials, and every individual intervention available to him only recovered by leaving the country—what does that say about our approaches to depression? What does it say about systems that create depression faster than we can treat it?

This book will make some colleagues uncomfortable. It questions the medical model we've built careers on. It challenges the pharmaceutical approaches that dominate treatment. It suggests that much of what we call mental illness might be environmental mismatch requiring systemic solutions rather than individual interventions.

Some will dismiss it as anti-psychiatry or anti-medication or politically motivated. It's none of those things. It's anti-bullshit, which is different and considerably more useful.

Lee doesn't argue against medication—he argues against using medication as first-line treatment for systemic problems. He doesn't dismiss individual therapy—he questions why we need so much of it. He doesn't deny chemical imbalances exist—he asks why we assume they're the primary cause when evidence suggests otherwise.

These are questions we should be asking ourselves.

I don't agree with everything in this book. Lee would be disappointed if I did—he's a contrarian who questions his own arguments as rigorously as everyone else's. But I agree with enough of it to believe this conversation is essential, and that we've avoided having it for too long because it's uncomfortable and threatens professional territory and suggests we might need to do our jobs differently.

What makes this book valuable isn't that Lee has all the answers—he explicitly doesn't, and tells you so repeatedly. It's that he's asking the right questions from a position of lived experience combined with academic rigour and clinical expertise. He's earned the authority to question systems that most of us accept without examination.

He's also Australian, which means he'll take the piss out of himself and everyone else whilst making serious points about serious problems. If you're looking for academic detachment or clinical formality, you've picked the wrong book. If you're looking for honest conversation about why so many people are depressed despite living in wealthy countries with advanced healthcare, keep reading.

This book won't tell you how to fix your depression through individual effort. That's not its purpose. It'll suggest your depression might be reasonable, your circumstances might be unreasonable, and systems might need changing more than your brain does.

Whether that's hopeful or depressing probably depends on your circumstances.

Read it anyway.

Gaye Idec, psychologist

Brisbane, 3rd October 2025

Chapter 1
The reasonable response

The car park revelation

I was sitting in my car in a Bunnings car park in Gawler at 3am on a Tuesday.

The hot water system had finally died. Not gradually—spectacularly. With the sort of mechanical violence that suggested it had been planning this betrayal for months.

I'd been lying awake listening to it die, and somewhere around 2am I'd had absolute clarity about my situation.

I couldn't afford to fix it. Couldn't afford to keep living in circumstances that kept requiring money I didn't have.

Couldn't afford to keep existing.

So I'd driven to Bunnings—because of course it would be Bunnings—and spent the past hour doing calculations.

Not about hot water systems. About exit strategies.

I'd already found the perfect location. Remote. Quiet. Carbon monoxide poisoning, straightforward enough. I'd written notes, organised what little needed organising. Done everything a responsible suicide ought to do.

Everything except check the fuel gauge.

Here's where the universe's questionable sense of humour really shines: I didn't have enough petrol to reach my carefully selected location.

I had $47 in my account until pension day. Petrol to my suicide location would cost approximately $55.

The mathematics were unkind.

I sat there doing calculations. Could I drive very slowly? Coast downhill sections? Find a closer location?

Then I started laughing. The slightly unhinged laughter of someone who's just realised they're too poor to afford dying.

Life is what happens when you're too poor to commit suicide.

That's when something occurred to me: maybe I wasn't the problem.

Maybe my brain wasn't broken. Maybe the circumstances were broken, and my brain was responding entirely reasonably to unreasonable circumstances.

Revolutionary, I know.

The story we've been sold

For forty years, we've been sold a specific story about depression.

Depression is a chemical imbalance. You don't have enough serotonin. Here's a pill. Problem solved.

Tidy. Medical. Scientific-sounding.

Also not actually supported by evidence.

In 2022, Joanna Moncrieff and colleagues published a systematic umbrella review examining the serotonin theory. They looked at decades of research. Every possible angle.

Their conclusion: there is no convincing evidence that depression is caused by lower serotonin.

Not "the evidence is mixed." The evidence doesn't support it.

The chemical imbalance theory—the foundation for forty years of depression treatment—is not supported by research.

Let me be clear: I'm not saying antidepressants don't help some people. They do. If medication helps you, take it without shame.

What I'm saying is the explanation for why they help—the tidy "chemical imbalance" story—doesn't hold up.

Which raises an interesting question: if it's not primarily a chemical imbalance, what is it?

The work nobody talks about

I'm a psychologist. Master's in Counselling Practice. I've worked primarily with veterans experiencing depression—people who served their country and got systematically betrayed afterwards.

I've sat across from hundreds of people told their brains were broken.

And I've watched what actually helps.

Not gratitude journals. Not cognitive restructuring. Not mindfulness. Not positive psychology. Not crystals and realigning my chakra. Not going barefoot into a forest and chanting.

What helps is when circumstances change.

When James finally got his disability claim approved after three years of appeals, his depression lifted within weeks. Not because his serotonin increased. Because he could pay rent without panic attacks.

When Sarah got her autism diagnosis after forty years of being told she was just difficult, her depression transformed overnight. Not because her neurotransmitters rebalanced. Because she could finally stop pretending to be someone she wasn't.

When Michael's workplace agreed to reasonable adjustments instead of performance-managing him out, his depression became manageable. Not because his brain changed. Because the daily torture stopped.

I wonder why that is.

(I'm lying. I know exactly why.)

The evidence we ignore

After the Berlin Wall fell, researchers could examine what happened to mental health when circumstances changed dramatically.

East Germans experienced significant improvements in mental health.

Not because they practiced gratitude. Not because they challenged negative thoughts about communist rule.

Because the circumstances making them unwell ended.

The brain didn't change. The circumstances did.

Or consider unemployment and depression. When people lose employment, depression increases. When they gain employment, it decreases.

Not because employment produces serotonin. Because having income changes your daily reality.

Or poverty and mental health. Or housing instability. Or discrimination.

The evidence is everywhere: when circumstances are hostile to human flourishing, humans stop flourishing.

We've just been very dedicated to ignoring it.

James and the gratitude journal

James came to see me in 2019. Ex-Army, early fifties, depressed for fifteen years.

He'd tried various antidepressants. Some helped a bit, most didn't.

He'd done therapy with three psychologists. They all taught the same approach: identify negative thoughts, challenge them, practice gratitude, exercise, sleep well, keep trying.

James did all of it. Religiously.

He kept a gratitude journal for six years. He could recite CBT principles better than most therapists. He exercised four times a week. He maintained perfect sleep hygiene.

He was still depressed.

'I must be doing it wrong,' he told me. 'Everyone says if you do the work, you get better.'

I asked him about his circumstances.

He lived in a one-bedroom flat. The military pension—$1,000 per fortnight—didn't quite cover rent plus food plus utilities. He was $80 short every fortnight.

He'd stopped seeing friends because he couldn't afford to go out. Stopped browsing shops because browsing without buying felt like torture. Spent most of his time at home, trying to be grateful for increasingly minimal things.

His brain wasn't the problem. The circumstances were.

We worked together for eighteen months. Not on his thoughts—on his circumstances.

We got him connected with veterans' advocacy groups. Found free community activities. Worked on practical problems like how to survive poverty whilst everyone tells you the problem is your attitude.

His depression didn't vanish. But it became manageable.

Not because his thinking changed. Because his circumstances improved enough that his brain could stop screaming about survival threats.

Psychological contracts and broken promises

There's a concept called the psychological contract. The unwritten expectations between employers and employees.

When organisations violate these contracts—when promises turn out to be suggestions—the psychological damage is profound.

My research on this earned over 1,200 citations. Which just means 1,200 people thought I said something relevant enough to mention, even if they disagreed with me.

Here's what occurred to me at 3am in that car park: society has a psychological contract too.

Work hard, follow rules, contribute to society—and you'll be rewarded with security, dignity, healthcare, liveable income.

What happens when that contract is systematically violated?

When you serve your country and receive a pension below poverty line? When you do everything right but still end up unable to afford petrol to your planned suicide?

The standard answer: adjust your thinking. Practice gratitude. Take medication. Try harder.

Maybe the problem is your attitude about being betrayed?

But what if that's just sophisticated gaslighting? Stop noticing the system is broken. Stop trusting your accurate perception of betrayal. Start believing the story we need you to believe.

Because if people recognised their depression was a reasonable response to systemic problems, they might demand systemic solutions.

That would be terribly inconvenient.

The Vietnam experiment

I moved to Vietnam in May 2025. Sixty-six years old, convinced I had chronic mental illness I'd manage until I died.

Within two months, my depression lifted.

Just lifted.

Same brain. Same neurotransmitters. Same genes. Same bloke who months earlier couldn't afford petrol to his planned suicide.

My photography changed first. In Adelaide, I shot moody, melancholic black-and-white landscapes. Bleak. Empty. In Vietnam, colour returned. Vibrant portraits. Street life. The same camera, completely different output.

Then my mood followed.

I'd like to present neat evidence for why Vietnam worked. But truth is messier.

What I know: my Australian pension goes four times further here. I can afford to live comfortably. The sensory environment is manageable. The social expectations suit my neurology better. The masking requirements are reduced.

Same pension. Different cost of living. Everything changed.

Was it the money? The culture? The environment? Simply time?

Maybe I was going to improve anyway and Vietnam just happened to be where I was.

I don't know.

What I know with certainty: the same brain that couldn't function in Adelaide functions fine here.

Which makes me wonder: was the problem ever really my brain?

Or was it that my brain couldn't survive in circumstances that would crush anyone?

What the research actually shows

When you look at actual research on depression—not pharmaceutical marketing, but peer-reviewed evidence—a pattern emerges.

Depression correlates consistently with adverse circumstances. Poverty. Unemployment. Housing instability. Chronic illness. Discrimination. Social isolation.

Not perfectly. Some people experience adversity without depression. Some develop depression in good circumstances.

But the correlation is strong enough to make us question whether the problem is primarily brain chemistry or environmental circumstances.

Depression might be less like diabetes—internal malfunction requiring external correction—and more like an alarm system. Alerting you that something is wrong around you, not in you.

The solution isn't turning off the alarm. It's addressing what triggered it.

The question nobody asked

I spent decades being treated for depression. Medication. Therapy. Hospitalisation. ECT—they actually ran electricity through my brain.

Nobody ever asked if circumstances might be the problem.

Nobody asked if my brain was responding reasonably to unreasonable circumstances.

Nobody suggested the solution might be changing my situation, not adjusting my brain until it tolerated the situation.

They just kept trying to fix my brain.

Rather elegant. In a dystopian sort of way.

Medicalise the symptoms, send people back into toxic circumstances. If you can convince people their suffering is medical, you don't have to address systemic problems creating the suffering.

I wonder why systems prefer that approach.

(I'm lying again.)

The veteran's pension

I served in the RAAF. Did what my country asked. Was shot at. Was honourably discharged.

My Disability Pension is $1,000 per fortnight. Approximately $26,000 per year.

The poverty line in Australia is roughly $26,000 per year for a single person.

The Australian government pays veterans below the poverty line once you factor in the cost of medicines, the cost of transport to and from medical appointments, the cost of living.

Then wonders why so many veterans experience depression.

It's like locking someone in a room full of snakes then offering them excellent CBT for their fear of snakes.

The fear isn't the problem. The snakes are the problem.

A framework that makes sense

Through working with veterans, through my own experience, I've developed a framework.

Depression happens when four conditions align:

First: Adverse circumstances—poverty, isolation, discrimination, chronic stress, trauma. Situations genuinely hostile to human flourishing.

Second: Insufficient resources to change those circumstances or cope adequately.

Third: Learned helplessness—well-founded belief that nothing you do will change circumstances. Not pessimism. Realism about systemic constraints.

Fourth: No viable exit—can't leave the job, relationship, country, poverty. Can't change fundamental conditions.

When those align, depression follows.

Not because your brain is broken. Because your brain is doing what it should—alerting you to danger, conserving energy, protecting you from consequences of hope when hope would be dangerous.

Your brain is working perfectly. The circumstances are broken.

What this book is about

This book questions the story we've been told about depression.

It examines whether the problem is primarily in our brains or our circumstances. It looks at systems creating mass suffering, then medicalising symptoms.

It's about my journey from decades of depression in Australia to unexpected recovery in Vietnam. Not as a solution everyone should copy, but as evidence that the same brain functions differently in different environments.

It's about research supporting systemic understanding of depression. About clients whose depression lifted when circumstances changed. About questioning whether we're treating the right thing.

I'm not offering certainty. I'm offering questions based on research, clinical experience, and forty years living with depression.

I'm suggesting maybe your brain is working exactly as it should. Maybe the problem is circumstances fundamentally hostile to human flourishing.

Permission to trust yourself

If you've been told your brain is broken but suspect circumstances are the problem—you might be right.

If medication helps you function, that's valid. But you don't have to accept your brain is broken. You can take medication whilst acknowledging your brain might be responding reasonably to unreasonable situations.

If therapy helps, that's valuable. But you don't have to blame yourself for needing coping strategies. You can learn to cope whilst recognising the problem isn't your inability to cope—it's circumstances requiring constant coping.

If you've tried everything and you're still depressed, you're not failing. Circumstances might genuinely be the problem.

Trust your experience.

The exhaustion I didn't mention

There's a specific tiredness I haven't mentioned yet.

Not from working hard. Not even depression tiredness, exactly.

The tiredness from pretending to be someone you're not. From performing normalcy when your brain runs on different operating system than society expects.

I was sixty-six when I got my autism and ADHD diagnoses.

Everything suddenly made sense—and nothing in therapy had ever addressed it.

Understanding that the chemical imbalance theory doesn't hold up should be liberating. Should make you question everything you've been told about why you feel the way you feel.

For me, it raised a different question entirely.

If it wasn't primarily brain chemistry making me depressed for decades, what was it? What had I been fighting against all those years whilst thinking I was fighting my own neurology?

The answer, when it finally came at sixty-six, reframed my entire life in ways that were simultaneously infuriating and profoundly relieving.

Turns out I'd been exhausted for a very specific reason that had nothing to do with serotonin and everything to do with spending sixty-six years pretending to be someone I wasn't.

References

Moncrieff, J., Cooper, R. E., Stockmann, T., Amendola, S., Hengartner, M. P., & Horowitz, M. A. (2022). The serotonin theory of depression: A systematic umbrella review of the evidence. *Molecular Psychiatry, 28*(8), 3243-3256.

Paul, K. I., & Moser, K. (2009). Unemployment impairs mental health: Meta-analyses. *Journal of Vocational Behavior, 74*(3), 264-282.

Sapolsky, R. M. (2004). *Why zebras don't get ulcers: The acclaimed guide to stress, stress-related diseases, and coping*. Henry Holt and Company.

Chapter 2
The masking exhaustion

The tiredness that sleep doesn't touch

There's a specific tiredness that comes from spending sixteen hours pretending to be someone you're not.

Not the honest exhaustion of physical labour. Not even the mental fatigue of complex problem-solving.

Different.

This exhaustion seeps into your bones and sets up permanent residence. It accumulates day after day, year after year, until you can't remember what it feels like to simply exist without constant effort.

Like tinnitus, but for your entire nervous system.

I spent sixty-six years experiencing that tiredness without having a name for it.

Then I got diagnosed with AuDHD—autism and ADHD occurring together, which apparently makes me a limited-edition collector's item in the neurodivergent community.

Suddenly, decades of inexplicable exhaustion made perfect sense.

I hadn't been lazy. Hadn't been weak. Hadn't been suffering from mysterious chronic fatigue.

I'd been masking.

And masking is absolutely fucking exhausting.

The twenty-four-hour performance

Imagine you're an actor in a play that runs twenty-four hours a day, seven days a week, with no intermission and definitely no union representation.

You have to stay in character constantly. One slip and people notice. They give you that look—something's not quite right about you, can't put my finger on what.

So you don't slip.

You monitor every word, every gesture, every facial expression. You watch other people constantly, taking notes on how they interact. You develop scripts for common situations. You rehearse conversations before they happen.

All of this happens automatically, beneath conscious awareness, because you learned it so young you don't remember learning.

Until one day your body sends you a bill for decades of constant performance.

The bill arrives marked "URGENT: PAYMENT OVERDUE."

We call that bill depression.

But I wonder if it's depression at all, or just the predictable outcome of running your nervous system at maximum capacity for forty, fifty, sixty years without a tea break.

The diagnosis at sixty-six

I was sixty-six when a psychologist—younger than my shoes, irritatingly perceptive—said the words that reframed my entire life.

'Have you thought you might be neurodivergent?'

My first response was to laugh. Proper guffaw.

Autism? ADHD? Those were diagnosed in children. Hyperactive boys who couldn't sit still. Kids who lined up toys obsessively.

I'd been a RAAF serviceman. Run businesses—unsuccessfully, but still. Earned a research degree. Practised as a psychologist for decades.

How could I possibly be autistic?

'High-masking,' she explained. 'People who learn to compensate so well they pass as neurotypical. Often diagnosed late, if at all.'

She handed me a screening questionnaire.

I scored in the "extremely likely" range for both.

Felt rather like being told you've been playing tennis your entire life whilst everyone else was playing cricket.

The informal assessment confirmed it. AuDHD. Autism and ADHD together. Custom firmware nobody mentioned in the documentation.

An informal assessment because I couldn't afford to have a psychiatrist confirm what science and my own lived experience were shouting at me.

Everything suddenly made sense

The diagnosis didn't change my brain. My brain had always been autistic.

The diagnosis changed my understanding of why everything had been so hard.

Why small talk felt like complex mathematics requiring constant calculation.

Why networking events left me destroyed for days.

Why I needed absolute silence and darkness to recover from social interaction.

Why unexpected changes felt catastrophic rather than merely inconvenient.

Why I'd failed at business after business—not because I lacked skill but because I couldn't do the endless social lubrication that business requires.

Why my photography was technically perfect but emotionally distant.

Why depression had been my constant companion since childhood. Why I had faked my own suicide at seven years old.

None of this was character flaw. None of it was lack of effort.

It was neurodivergence in a neurotypical world.

What therapy never addressed

I've done decades of therapy. CBT. Interpersonal. ACT. Schema. DBT. Psychodynamic. I've probably tried therapeutic approaches that haven't been invented yet.

Not once did any therapist suggest that perhaps the problem wasn't my thoughts or behaviours or inability to regulate emotions.

Perhaps the problem was trying to function in environments designed for brains that work differently than mine.

Instead, therapy taught me to be better at masking. To identify "maladaptive" thoughts—translation: neurotypical brains don't think this way. To practice "appropriate" social behaviours—translation: do what neurotypical people do even though it exhausts you.

Therapy made me better at pretending to be neurotypical.

It did not make me less exhausted.

The research on masking and mental health

The research on autistic masking and mental health is fairly devastating.

High-masking autistic adults show significantly elevated rates of depression, anxiety, and suicidality compared to low-masking autistic adults.

Masking requires constant cognitive effort. That effort is exhausting. The exhaustion is cumulative. The cumulative exhaustion creates vulnerability to mental health difficulties.

And here's the thing: masking develops as survival strategy in childhood. You learn quickly that being authentic leads to bullying, exclusion, punishment.

So you learn to hide. You get very good at hiding.

By the time you're an adult, masking is automatic. You don't even realise you're doing it.

But your nervous system knows.

Sarah's story

Sarah came to see me for depression in 2020. She was forty-seven. Diagnosed with depression at twenty-three, on antidepressants for twenty-four years.

She was meticulous in our sessions. Prepared notes. Answered questions thoughtfully. Maintained appropriate eye contact—just slightly too consistently.

I asked her, during our fourth session, whether she'd ever considered that she might be autistic.

She went completely still. 'Why would you ask that?'

'Because you look exhausted. And not depression-tired. You look masking-tired.'

She started crying. Not delicate tears. Proper sobbing. Twenty-four years of exhaustion coming out all at once.

We worked on getting her an autism assessment. The diagnosis was clear.

Within six months of receiving her diagnosis and starting to unmask in safe spaces, her depression began to lift.

The problem wasn't primarily her brain chemistry. The problem was spending forty-seven years pretending to be someone she wasn't.

Military service as masking boot camp

The RAAF was, in retrospect, both worst and best environment for an undiagnosed autistic person.

Worst because military culture requires conformity, social bonding, unwritten hierarchical rules. All the things that exhaust autistic brains.

Best because it also provides clear rules, explicit hierarchies, structured routines. All the things that help autistic brains function.

I was good at military service in many ways. I followed rules precisely. Maintained routines religiously. Mastered technical skills.

I was terrible at military service in other ways. The informal social hierarchy confused me. The mateship culture required constant socialising that destroyed me.

The RAAF taught me discipline and resilience and how to function under pressure.

But it also taught me that my natural way of being was a liability to be hidden at all costs.

That lesson shaped the next forty years.

The three failed businesses

I started three businesses over twenty years. Not one succeeded.

Each failure felt deeply personal. Evidence of inadequacy. Inability to make right decisions.

I watched other people start businesses and thrive. Read books about entrepreneurship that made it sound straightforward.

It wasn't straightforward for me.

Networking events left me drained for days. The constant context-switching felt like being forced to stop mid-sentence, over and over. The open-ended nature of entrepreneurship suited my ADHD brain until it didn't, and then I couldn't force myself to focus on boring administrative tasks even when essential.

Business advice was always the same: network more, market yourself, be visible, follow up consistently.

All perfectly reasonable advice for neurotypical brains.

All utterly exhausting for mine.

Eventually I gave up on entrepreneurship. Told myself I wasn't cut out for it.

Now I understand: I was trying to run businesses designed for neurotypical operating systems on neurodivergent hardware.

The businesses didn't fail because I was inadequate. They failed because the entire entrepreneurial ecosystem assumes neurotypical functioning.

The expensive burden of masking

Here's something nobody tells you: masking is expensive.

When you're neurodivergent, you need accommodations just to function at the level neurotypical people achieve naturally. Those accommodations cost money.

You need quiet workspace? That's extra rent.

You need to live alone because housemates overwhelm you? Double the housing cost.

You need prepared meals because executive dysfunction means you forget to eat? Expensive.

You need taxis because public transport overwhelms you? That adds up fast.

But if you're poor—as I was for many years—you can't afford accommodations that would reduce masking load.

You live in housing that's too loud or too chaotic. You work in environments hostile to your nervous system. You don't have option to take breaks.

So you mask harder, which makes you more exhausted, which tanks your performance, which makes you poorer, which forces you into worse circumstances, which requires more masking.

It's a vicious cycle that looks exactly like depression.

But it's not depression. It's poverty whilst neurodivergent.

The hell of high-masking

Here's the particular hell of high-masking neurodivergence: you've trained yourself so thoroughly to appear normal that when you try to explain you're struggling, nobody believes you.

'But you seem fine.'

'You're holding down a job, though.'

'Everyone gets a bit overwhelmed sometimes.'

The very fact that you've succeeded in masking is used as evidence that you don't need accommodations.

This is the Catch-22 of high-masking: you're disabled enough to struggle constantly, but not disabled enough for anyone to recognise your struggles as legitimate.

You fall through every gap in the support system. Too functional for disability services. Too disabled to compete equally.

Constantly performing at 200% capacity just to achieve 80% of neurotypical outcomes, and having everyone assume you're lazy because they only see the 80%.

It's like running a marathon whilst everyone else walks to the shops, but because you're keeping up, they assume you're also walking and wonder why you're so tired.

What masking exhaustion actually felt like

Let me describe what masking exhaustion felt like before I had words for it.

Every morning, I'd wake up already tired. Not sleepy—tired. Like my nervous system had been running at full capacity all night.

Getting ready for work required conscious decisions about everything neurotypical people do automatically. How much eye contact? What facial expression? Is this outfit acceptable?

The workday was constant performance. Monitoring voice tone, maintaining appropriate expressions, participating in conversations that felt like learning a foreign language through immersion.

By 3pm, I'd be running on fumes. Every interaction took conscious effort. Every unexpected change felt catastrophic.

Coming home meant collapse. Not relaxation—collapse. Lying in the dark, unable to engage with anything, too exhausted even for activities I normally enjoyed.

And the next day would be exactly the same.

This continued for years. Decades.

I accepted it as normal because I'd never known anything different.

The doctors called it depression.

It wasn't depression. It was masking exhaustion.

The photography evidence

Getting diagnosed with AuDHD at sixty-six had unexpected benefits.

I could look back and see patterns I'd missed whilst living through them.

My photography documented this shift in real time, though I didn't understand what I was seeing.

In Adelaide, under constant financial pressure, trying to build businesses that didn't suit my neurology, masking constantly—my perception narrowed. Everything was muted.

The world looked grey. Flat. Empty.

In Vietnam, with financial pressure reduced, living in a culture that suited my natural communication style better, no longer forcing myself into entrepreneurial moulds—my perception opened back up.

The world had colour again.

Same camera. Same technical skills. Completely different perception of reality.

You can track my nervous system recovery through my photography archive.

This is what reduced masking load looks like when you document it accidentally.

The question every professional should ask

Here's the question I wish every mental health professional would ask before reaching for depression diagnosis and prescription pad:

'Have you ever wondered if you might be neurodivergent?'

Not 'Do you have autism?' Because high-masking people will say no.

Just: 'Have you ever wondered if your brain might work differently?'

Because neurodivergent people know, on some level, that they're different. They've spent their whole lives feeling out of step. They've developed elaborate strategies to compensate without understanding what they're compensating for.

That wondering is usually dismissed. 'Everyone feels different sometimes.'

But what if it's accurate perception that you're running different software, and that software wasn't designed for the operating system everyone assumes you have?

I wonder how many people diagnosed with depression would be better served by autism and ADHD assessment.

I don't have data to answer definitively. But in my clinical practice, once I started asking that question, I found neurodivergence everywhere I'd previously seen treatment-resistant depression.

Everywhere.

What the diagnosis gave me

Getting diagnosed at sixty-six didn't give me my years back. Didn't undo decades of struggle or misguided treatment.

But it gave me understanding.

For the first time, I had a framework that made sense. I wasn't broken or weak or insufficient. I was neurodivergent in a neurotypical world.

More importantly, I could distinguish between problems about my neurology and problems about my circumstances.

The depression in Adelaide wasn't just masking exhaustion—it was also poverty, financial stress, business failures, cultural mismatch, pension betrayal.

The recovery in Vietnam wasn't just reduced masking—it was also financial breathing room, cultural fit, environmental change.

Understanding my neurology didn't negate systemic issues. It clarified them.

And clarity is powerful.

Because once you understand what's actually happening, you can start making strategic choices instead of just suffering through circumstances you assume are inevitable.

When systems become the enemy

I spent decades being crushed by systems designed for neurotypical brains.

Open-plan offices that made concentration impossible. Fluorescent lighting that caused sensory pain. Social expectations requiring constant masking. Interview processes penalising autistic communication. Workplace cultures rewarding face time over output.

Every accommodation was framed as special exception to normal expectations.

Never mind that "normal expectations" were created by and for neurotypical brains. Never mind that approximately 15-25% of the population is neurodivergent. Never mind that systems could accommodate diversity by default.

The framing reinforces the idea that neurotypical design is natural and neutral, whilst neurodivergent needs are special demands.

What if we flipped that? What if we designed workplaces for variety of neurologies by default?

Then neurodivergent workers wouldn't need to identify themselves and request accommodations. They could just work in environments that suited them.

But that would require acknowledging our systems are designed for only one type of brain.

So instead we keep treating neurodivergent exhaustion as depression and offering medication to help individuals adjust to systems fundamentally inhospitable to their neurology.

And we wonder why so many people are depressed.

So I was neurodivergent in a neurotypical world, exhausted from decades of masking, and everyone had been treating it as depression.

Which explained a lot.

But it didn't explain everything.

Because even after understanding my neurodivergence, even after recognising the masking exhaustion, I was still depressed in Adelaide. Still lying awake at 3am. Still unable to afford apples without existential crisis.

The neurodivergence was real. The masking exhaustion was real.

But there was something else happening too. Something broader. Something that affected everyone trapped in similar circumstances, neurotypical or not.

I'd spent decades working with veterans who weren't neurodivergent but were experiencing exactly the same crushing despair I was. Same circumstances. Same systemic betrayal. Same reasonable responses being treated as individual pathology.

Which made me wonder: what happens when the systems meant to support you are actually designed to crush you? When the institutions promising care deliver abandonment instead? When bureaucracy becomes a weapon deployed against people who need help?

Let me tell you about sixteen hours and thirty-seven minutes on hold with Centrelink, and what that teaches us about systems that create depression whilst blaming individuals for being depressed.

References

Cage, E., & Troxell-Whitman, Z. (2019). Understanding the reasons, contexts and costs of camouflaging for autistic adults. *Journal of Autism and Developmental Disorders, 49*(5), 1899-1911.

Hull, L., Petrides, K. V., Allison, C., Smith, P., Baron-Cohen, S., Lai, M. C., & Mandy, W. (2017). "Putting on my best normal": Social camouflaging in adults with autism spectrum conditions. *Journal of Autism and Developmental Disorders, 47*(8), 2519-2534.

Hull, L., Levy, L., Lai, M. C., Petrides, K. V., Baron-Cohen, S., Allison, C., Smith, P., & Mandy, W. (2021). Is social camouflaging associated with anxiety and depression in autistic adults? *Molecular Autism, 12*(1), 13.

Chapter 3
When systems fail

Sixteen hours and thirty-seven minutes

I once spent sixteen hours and thirty-seven minutes on hold with Centrelink.

I know the exact time because I started tracking it like some people track bird sightings—a hobby born of desperation and too much time listening to hold music composed by someone who'd never heard music but had it described to them once at a party.

Sixteen hours across multiple calls. Each one a small journey into bureaucratic underworld.

Ring the number. Navigate the automated system designed by someone who clearly harboured deep resentment towards human communication. Listen to cheerful recorded voice insist your call was important to them. Wait. Get disconnected at the exact moment you think you might be getting somewhere.

Start again.

By the third attempt, I'd developed a relationship with the hold music. Started recognising loops. Found myself humming along. Wondered if this was Stockholm syndrome.

I was ringing about my disability pension, which had stopped arriving without warning or explanation.

One week it was there. Next fortnight, nothing. Just digital tumbleweed rolling through my bank account.

When I finally spoke to an actual human—and I say "human" with uncertainty because by that point I'd started wondering if they were sophisticated chatbots—they informed me my pension had been "suspended pending review."

'What review?'

'I can't access that information.'

'When will it be completed?'

'I can't access that information either.'

'So my pension has been stopped for reasons you can't tell me, for a duration you can't specify, and there's nothing I can do?'

'You can lodge an appeal.'

'How long does an appeal take?'

'I can't access—'

I hung up.

The pension reappeared four weeks later with no explanation, no apology, no back-payment. Just suddenly there again, like a cat that's been out all night and refuses to explain where it's been.

Four weeks without income when you're living on $1,000 per fortnight is the sort of event that reorganises your entire nervous system.

And the entire time, I was meant to maintain my mental health whilst navigating a system seemingly designed to create maximum psychological distress with minimum institutional accountability.

This is what I mean when I say systems fail.

The gaslighting after violation

Here's something interesting about psychological contract violations: the violation isn't the worst part.

The worst part is the gaslighting that follows.

When employers breach psychological contracts, they rarely say 'Yes, we broke our promise and we're sorry.'

Instead, they reframe it. Language so smooth it could be used as lubricant.

'We're all having to be more flexible in this challenging economic climate.'

'Are you really committed to being a team player?'

The subtext is clear: there's no contract violation because there was never really a contract. You imagined it. You're being unreasonable.

Governments do exactly the same thing, just with more flags.

Society promises: serve your country, we'll take care of you. Work hard, you'll have security.

Then when those promises are systematically broken, the response isn't 'We're sorry we broke our promise.'

It's 'You should be grateful for what you get.'

'Others have it worse.'

'If you'd worked harder, you wouldn't need help.'

The gaslight flickers whilst you freeze in the dark.

The customer service charter

The Department of Veterans' Affairs has a customer service charter that promises to treat veterans with respect and dignity whilst processing claims efficiently and fairly.

I've read it multiple times, usually whilst on hold.

The charter is beautifully written. Inspiring. Makes you feel valued and heard.

Right until you actually try to access services.

At which point you discover "efficiently and fairly" apparently means "with maximum bureaucratic obstruction," rather like promising someone a sandwich and delivering two slices of bread with a photo of ham between them.

Getting my disability pension approved took eighteen months.

Eighteen months of forms asking the same questions in slightly different ways. Eighteen months of medical assessments where doctors who'd never met me decided whether I was sufficiently damaged. Eighteen months of proving, over and over, that I had indeed served.

At one point I genuinely wondered if I should get "I REALLY DID SERVE, I PROMISE" tattooed on my forehead.

The process is exhausting by design, I suspect.

If accessing benefits is difficult enough, some people give up. Every person who gives up is money saved.

From a treasury perspective, that's brilliant.

From a human perspective, it's monstrous.

But systems don't optimise for human wellbeing. They optimise for whatever metrics they're measured on.

Possibly with cake.

Exhaustion by design

I once asked a Centrelink case worker why the process was so complicated.

'Well,' she said carefully, 'we have to make sure people really need it.'

'As opposed to all those people who enjoy spending eighteen months completing paperwork for sheer pleasure?'

She laughed, then caught herself.

But here's what that means: the system assumes you're lying until you prove otherwise.

You're not a veteran who served your country and deserves support. You're a potential fraudster requiring thorough investigation.

Guilty until proven innocent, except the proof required keeps shifting out of reach, and the process of providing it is designed to make you give up.

Rather like being asked to prove you're not a swan whilst people keep moving the goalposts and also what even is a swan really?

Michael's story

Michael came to see me during my clinical practice. Forty-three. Former warehouse worker. Had injured his back at work three years earlier.

Not dramatically. Just cumulative damage from years lifting heavy objects in awkward positions because the warehouse valued productivity over proper equipment.

His back never healed. Chronic pain, limited mobility, unable to return to manual labour.

He'd been on worker's compensation initially. Then the insurance company decided he should be "recovered" by now and cut him off.

Never mind that his back was still injured. The insurance company had a table that said eighteen months was sufficient recovery time.

Tables don't argue back.

He'd applied for disability support. Been rejected. Applied again. Rejected. Appealed. Rejected.

Currently he was on JobSeeker, which required him to apply for twenty jobs per month despite having documented disability preventing him from doing most work.

Twenty job applications per month. Each one a small humiliation. Each rejection proof—in his mind—that he was worthless.

'I'm not depressed,' he told me flatly. 'I'm just tired of pretending there's a point to any of this.'

His GP had diagnosed major depressive disorder. Tried several antidepressants. None made Michael feel better about being forced to apply for jobs he couldn't do to receive a benefit that didn't cover rent.

'What would you do,' I asked, 'if you had enough money to live on without working, and nobody was forcing you to pretend?'

He stared at me like I'd suggested he grow wings and fly to the moon.

'That's not a real option.'

'Hypothetically.'

He thought about it. 'I'd volunteer at the community garden. I can't do heavy lifting, but I could do planning, coordinate volunteers, teach kids about growing vegetables.'

'So you want to contribute. You just can't do it through traditional employment because your back is fundamentally opposed to lifting things.'

'Yeah. But that's not how the system works. If you can't work—like, paid work in a proper job—you're just worthless. A drain.'

And there it was.

Michael wasn't depressed because his brain had a chemical imbalance.

Michael was depressed because he was living in a system that treated him as worthless whilst forcing him to perform a degrading charade to receive inadequate support.

No amount of sertraline was going to fix that.

Process matters more than outcome

Here's what research on psychological contracts reveals about organisational justice: people can tolerate quite a lot of hardship if they believe the process is fair.

If redundancies are necessary but the process is transparent, people cope. If pay is modest but allocated fairly, people accept it.

The outcome matters less than the process.

But when the process is opaque, capricious, seemingly designed to maximise difficulty—that's when brains start sending distress signals that look exactly like depression.

And that's exactly how most social support systems in Australia operate.

Opaque processes where rules change arbitrarily. Decisions made without explanation by people you'll never meet. Appeals vanishing into bureaucratic black holes. Case workers changing so frequently you have to explain your situation repeatedly to people with no context.

Forms designed to be confusing. Waiting times stretching for months. Payments mysteriously stopping with no warning.

All creating the impression that whether you receive support is basically random chance combined with your ability to navigate deliberately obtuse systems.

That's not a bug. That's a feature.

The healthcare response

The healthcare system's response to systemically created depression would be hilarious if it weren't tragic.

Someone is depressed because they're poor, isolated, in chronic pain, trapped in circumstances they can't escape, navigating systems designed to exhaust them.

Healthcare's response: 'Have you tried medication?'

Not: 'Let's get you better housing.'

Not: 'Let's connect you with community support.'

Not: 'Let's help you navigate welfare systems.'

Not: 'Let's address the chronic pain.'

Just: 'Have you tried medication? No? Try this one. Doesn't work? Try this one.'

I've seen people cycle through five, seven, ten different antidepressants, each requiring weeks to determine if it works, each carrying side effects —weight gain, sexual dysfunction, emotional numbing. I am one of them.

Spoiler: it doesn't work.

Not because medication is bad. But because you can't medicate your way out of poverty. No amount of sertraline will make an abusive relationship safe or a soul-crushing job meaningful.

Sometimes medication provides breathing room to deal with circumstances. Like morphine doesn't fix a broken leg but makes the pain bearable enough to get help.

But the majority of people I saw were depressed for reasons medication couldn't touch.

They were depressed because they were poor in a society treating poverty as moral failure.

Because they were trapped in abusive relationships with no resources to leave.

Because they were caring for sick family with no help.

Because they were working jobs grinding them down whilst paying poverty wages.

Because they were dealing with chronic illness in a system providing inadequate support.

Because they were exhausted from navigating bureaucratic systems designed to make everything difficult.

Medication might help them feel slightly less terrible about terrible circumstances.

But it won't fix the circumstances.

Pretending it will serves everyone's interests except people who are suffering.

The institutional betrayal

I mentioned my pension mysteriously stopped for four weeks. What I didn't mention was what those four weeks did to my mental health.

The first week, I was annoyed but coping. Assuming it was an error.

The second week, anxiety set in. What if it didn't come back? What if I'd been removed from the system?

The third week, despair spirals. Lying awake at 3am calculating how long I could survive. Wondering if I should cancel internet to save forty dollars, but needing internet to access support services.

Going through possessions trying to figure out what I could sell.

This is what poverty does to your brain.

Not because your brain is malfunctioning. Because your brain is working exactly as designed—recognising threat, calculating survival odds, sending urgent distress signals.

When the pension returned—no explanation, just suddenly there again—the anxiety didn't immediately lift.

Because now I knew it could disappear at any moment without warning.

That uncertainty creates constant background stress that never quite goes away.

Like living next to a volcano that might erupt but doesn't feel obligated to give advance notice.

The psychological violence of means-testing

I need to tell you about the psychological violence of means-testing.

Means-testing is proving you're poor enough to deserve help.

It sounds reasonable. We have limited resources, give them to people who need them most.

But here's what it actually means:

You have to prove, repeatedly, that you have no money. Provide bank statements showing your poverty in precise detail. Asset declarations confirming you haven't hidden resources. Proof you haven't squirrelled away savings.

If you have savings above a threshold, you're ineligible until you've spent them down to nothing.

So the system actively prevents financial security. Any buffer. Any ability to handle unexpected expenses.

If someone gives you money, you have to declare it, and it might affect your payment.

So the system punishes people for having supportive relationships.

If you do casual work to supplement inadequate benefits, your payment is reduced dollar-for-dollar.

So the system creates poverty trap where working doesn't improve your situation.

The entire system is designed around the assumption that you must be constantly monitored, constantly verified, constantly proven to deserve minimal support.

And that constant surveillance, that perpetual need to prove your worthiness—that's psychological violence.

It creates exactly the conditions that generate depression: lack of control, constant uncertainty, degradation, chronic stress.

And then we wonder why people on welfare have high rates of mental illness.

What if we trusted people?

Here's what I wonder: what if we designed welfare systems that trusted people?

Universal basic income studies show something interesting: when you give people money with no strings attached, no surveillance, no degrading conditions—they don't become lazy.

They make better decisions.

They take time to retrain. They leave bad jobs for better ones. They start small businesses. They do unpaid care work. They volunteer. They create art.

And their mental health improves.

Not because money fixed their broken brains. Because money removed chronic stress and uncertainty and surveillance and degradation that were creating depression.

When people have security, they flourish.

When they lack security—when they're constantly on edge of disaster, constantly surveilled, constantly degraded—they deteriorate.

This isn't mysterious. It's not even surprising.

But acknowledging it would require acknowledging our systems actively harm people whilst blaming them for the harm.

The bottom line

Michael eventually gave up on disability support. Decided the process was too humiliating, too exhausting, too degrading.

Last I heard, he was still on JobSeeker, still applying for twenty jobs per month he can't do, still living in a system treating him as worthless.

Still depressed, obviously.

Still on medication that doesn't address the actual problem.

I think about Michael sometimes, here in Vietnam where systems are different—not perfect, but different in ways that accidentally suit me better.

I think about how many Michaels there are. How many people ground down by systems that could be designed differently but won't be.

And I wonder what would happen if we acknowledged that systemically created depression requires systemic solutions, not just individual treatment.

What if we looked at depression rates and asked: what are our systems doing to people?

Rather than: what's wrong with all these broken individuals?

Might be worth thinking about.

Michael's still out there somewhere, still trapped in systems grinding him down, still being told his reasonable response to unreasonable circumstances is a mental illness requiring pharmaceutical management.

And so are millions of others.

Systems fail. Institutions betray. Bureaucracies crush. We document it, research it, publish papers about it.

Then we treat the individuals being crushed rather than fixing the systems doing the crushing.

But here's what I kept coming back to, sitting in that Bunnings car park at 3am with insufficient petrol: it wasn't just the bureaucratic failures or institutional betrayals making me want to exit permanently.

It was something more immediate. More daily. More viscerally present in every single calculation I made.

I couldn't afford apples.

I owned a house and couldn't afford fruit.

That specific intersection of asset wealth and daily poverty—of technically owning things whilst unable to afford existence—creates its own particular despair that I need to tell you about.

Because poverty isn't what you think it is. And its relationship to depression is considerably more direct than anyone wants to acknowledge.

References

Fisher, M., & Baum, F. (2010). The social determinants of mental health: Implications for research and health promotion. *Australian & New Zealand Journal of Psychiatry, 44*(12), 1057-1063.

Friedli, L., & Stearn, R. (2015). Positive affect as coercive strategy: Conditionality, activation and the role of psychology in UK government workfare programmes. *Medical Humanities, 41*(1), 40-47.

Marmot, M., Allen, J., Goldblatt, P., Boyce, T., McNeish, D., Grady, M., & Geddes, I. (2010). *Fair society, healthy lives: The Marmot review*. London: The Marmot Review.

Chapter 4
Economic pressures

The apple calculation

I once stood in a supermarket aisle for twenty minutes trying to decide whether I could afford apples.

Not which variety. Not how many. Just whether apples existed in the category of "financially possible this week" or "things that happen to other people."

They were $4.99 per kilogram. Sounds reasonable until you're doing mathematics involving fruit purchases to the second decimal place whilst your soul slowly dies.

I had $47 left until pension day, three days away. House was sorted—rates paid, though that had required selling a kidney metaphorically. I needed bread, milk, something for protein that wasn't tinned tuna again because I'd eaten it four days straight and my body was staging a revolt.

Could I afford $3 for apples?

The mathematics said yes. The anxiety said no, because what if something unexpected came up? What if the hot water system finally died? What if there was a bill I'd forgotten?

$47 minus $3 for bread minus $4 for milk minus $8 for chicken thighs minus $3 for apples equals $29 left.

Should be enough unless the universe has other plans. Which it always does.

'Excuse me, mate,' someone said behind me, wanting to access the apples I was blocking whilst having an existential crisis about fruit affordability.

I moved aside without buying apples.

This is what poverty does to your brain.

The cognitive load of being poor

There's a concept researchers call "cognitive load of poverty."

Fancy way of saying: being poor is exhausting for your brain.

When you're poor, you're constantly making calculations that people with financial security never make.

Can I afford this? What if I buy this instead of that? If I skip this expense now, will it create a bigger expense later? Should I fix the leaking tap now or wait and hope it doesn't flood?

Every financial decision branches into multiple scenarios. Like playing chess except the pieces are your basic needs and the board is constantly tilting and possibly on fire.

A landmark study in *Science* gave people cognitive tests before and after creating artificial scarcity.

Same people performed significantly worse when feeling financially insecure.

Not because they'd become less intelligent. Because their cognitive resources were allocated to managing scarcity.

Another study found poverty reduces cognitive function by equivalent of 13 IQ points. That's roughly the difference between average intelligence and borderline intellectual disability.

Just from being poor.

Not permanently—give people financial security and their IQ points come back. But whilst you're poor, your brain literally functions worse.

And then we wonder why poor people make "bad decisions" or can't seem to get ahead.

They're playing chess on a tilting board whilst managing a cognitive handicap created by the very circumstances we're judging them for not escaping.

Brilliantly circular.

The Australian dream becomes a trap

Let me tell you about home ownership, which is supposed to be the Australian dream but turned out to be more of a recurring nightmare with property taxes.

When I returned from England in 1999 to look after my mother, I bought a house. Seemed sensible. I was in my forties, had savings, needed somewhere stable.

Less than a year later, I was made redundant. The payout was insulting —barely enough to cover a few months. Had to sell the house quickly.

"Desperate vendor will accept any offer" doesn't fetch good prices.

Took a loss. Suddenly starting over with less than before.

Next was my marital home, which lasted until 2017 when that arrangement dissolved. Then I moved into my mother's house after she died.

The house was slowly falling apart.

The roof leaked. Not spectacularly—persistently. The hot water system threatened to die every winter. Made ominous noises. The wiring was dubious. The plumbing spoke prophecies of doom.

Every time it rained, I'd lie awake wondering if this was the rain that would breach the roof properly. Every time I turned on hot water, I'd hold my breath.

Living in a house that's slowly failing around you whilst you can't afford to fix it is its own special poverty.

You own the property—technically, legally. But you don't have power to maintain it. You're just watching it deteriorate.

Like being given a pet that's dying slowly and you can't afford the vet bills but also can't afford to not have the pet because you need someone to love and love you back.

Asset rich, cash poor

In 2022, I sold my mother's house. Not because I wanted to. Because I had to.

The house needed work I couldn't afford—substantial work, tens of thousands. I could keep living in it whilst it deteriorated, waiting for something major to fail catastrophically.

Or I could sell whilst it was still sellable and buy something cheaper.

I bought a house in Gawler. Gawler is where people go when they can't afford Adelaide anymore. It's not bad. Just cheaper.

Cheaper house meant lower costs meant maybe I could stop lying awake worrying about appliances betraying me.

Three years in Gawler. Managing better but not thriving. Still calculating expenses, still choosing between things I needed.

Then I moved to Vietnam.

Here's what nobody tells you about home ownership when they're selling the Australian dream: it's a trap if you're poor.

"Renting is dead money," everyone says. Better to own. Build equity. Invest in your future.

Except when you're poor, home ownership means you're trapped with debt you can't escape and maintenance costs you can't afford.

At least with renting, when something breaks, you call the landlord. When you own and something breaks, you're just fucked.

I'm not saying home ownership is always a trap. If you have money, it's probably great.

But if you're poor, home ownership can chain you to a deteriorating asset that's simultaneously your shelter and your doom.

Three days without food

Let me tell you about the three days I had no food.

Not "no food I wanted." Actually no food.

This was eight months before I left Adelaide. Pension day was Friday. By Tuesday evening, I'd run out of everything edible.

Not through poor planning. An unexpected bill had eaten the buffer. Suddenly I was starring in my own famine except in suburban Gawler with considerably less historical significance.

Wednesday morning, I went through cupboards again. Found nothing except half a jar of Vegemite from the Howard government, expired tea bags, and possibly a fossilised stock cube.

Considered eating Vegemite straight but decided that was a level of desperation I hadn't reached yet. Also, eating Vegemite straight is morally questionable.

Wednesday afternoon, I told myself this was fine. Intermittent fasting, very trendy. The body could survive.

Wednesday evening, I stopped finding it philosophical. Lay in bed feeling hollow, trying to sleep because at least whilst sleeping you're not thinking about food.

Thursday morning, the hollow feeling evolved. Not quite pain. Constant awareness of absence.

Thursday afternoon, I seriously reconsidered the Vegemite. Stared at the jar for what felt like hours. Had internal debate about dignity versus survival.

Decided against it because eating Vegemite straight felt like admitting defeat in a way that just being hungry didn't.

Thursday evening, a friend rang to chat. I didn't mention I hadn't eaten in two days. What would be the point? They'd offer help, I'd feel ashamed, the whole interaction would become about my failure.

Also, I was a sixty-something former RAAF serviceman with a Master's degree. Admitting I couldn't afford food felt like admitting I'd failed at being an adult human.

Friday morning, pension arrived with all the glory of manna from heaven except less biblical.

Went to supermarket. Bought food. Real food. Multiple items.

Came home. Ate.

The relief wasn't pleasure exactly. More like pain stopping.

I felt ridiculous the entire time.

This was Australia. The lucky country. I was a military veteran on government pension, living in a house I owned.

But I was depressed.

And more importantly: I wasn't unique.

The research on poverty and mental health

The research on poverty and mental health is remarkably clear and remarkably ignored.

Multiple studies show financial stress is one of the strongest predictors of depression. Stronger than childhood trauma or personality traits or insufficient positive thinking.

A systematic review in *Clinical Psychology Review* found poverty and financial stress consistently associated with higher depression rates across cultures, age groups, study designs.

More poverty, more depression.

Revolutionary.

Another study tracked people over time. Found that entering poverty predicted new onset of depression. Escaping poverty predicted remission.

Even after controlling for personality, life history, genetics—poverty itself predicted depression.

Money might not buy happiness. But absence of money absolutely creates misery.

Yet somehow we've convinced ourselves poverty and mental health are separate issues. That depression is about brain chemistry rather than bank balances.

It's like expecting someone to be happy whilst standing in a burning building.

"Have you tried not noticing the fire?"

The vicious cycle

Here's something interesting about how poverty and depression interact: they create a vicious cycle almost impossible to escape.

Poverty creates depression through chronic stress, inadequate nutrition, poor housing, lack of healthcare access, social isolation, constant humiliation, cognitive load of managing scarcity.

Depression makes escaping poverty harder because it reduces energy, motivation, concentration, decision-making ability, capacity to perform cheerful competence that employers expect.

So poverty causes depression, which makes it harder to escape poverty, which worsens depression, which makes poverty harder to escape.

Round and round, like a terrible merry-go-round you can't afford to exit.

And then we tell people the solution is medication and therapy and positive thinking.

Without addressing the poverty creating and maintaining the depression.

It's like telling someone to think positively about drowning whilst leaving them in the water.

The business failures revisited

I started three businesses over twenty years. Each failed spectacularly.

I blamed myself. Assumed I lacked business acumen or entrepreneurial instinct.

Now I understand: I was trying to run businesses without capital whilst dealing with undiagnosed neurodivergence and poverty-induced depression in a system designed for people with money.

Every business book says you need financial runway. Need to survive months without income whilst building. Need to invest in marketing, equipment, professional development.

I had none of that.

I had to make money immediately or I couldn't pay rates on the house. Which meant I couldn't be selective. Couldn't invest in the business. Just had to grab whatever work came and hope it paid before the next bill.

Also trying to run businesses whilst dealing with undiagnosed AuDHD and poverty-induced depression didn't help.

But even if I'd been neurotypical and mentally healthy, I couldn't have succeeded without capital.

The businesses didn't fail because I was inadequate. They failed because I was poor, and poverty makes it nearly impossible to build wealth through entrepreneurship unless you start with wealth.

The rich get richer. Everyone else is told to manifest abundance.

The Vietnam solution

Moving to Vietnam didn't solve my poverty—I still have exactly the same pension.

But it solved poverty's consequences.

In Adelaide/Gawler, $1,000 per fortnight meant constant stress, impossible calculations, days without food.

In Đà Lạt, $1,000 per fortnight means modest comfort.

I rent here—haven't owned property since selling the Gawler house.

No maintenance costs. No rates. If something breaks, I call the landlord.

I pay $400 per month for a nice one-bedroom apartment. That leaves $1,200 for everything else. $300 per week.

Doesn't sound like much by Western standards. But here it covers food (actual food, not calculations about apples), utilities, transport, occasional dining out, healthcare, modest luxuries.

I'm not wealthy. But I'm not in poverty anymore.

Same income. Different cost of living. Everything changed.

The stress disappeared. The constant calculations stopped. I could buy apples without crisis. Go to a cafe and have a coffee in the presence of other humans. Could even have lunch or dinner with friends. Could afford to fix problems when small. Could think about things other than survival.

And miraculously—not miraculously at all, entirely predictably—my depression lifted.

Not because brain chemistry changed. Not because I found the right medication.

Because I escaped poverty.

What if we trusted people with money?

A universal basic income pilot in Finland gave people unconditional financial security.

Results: reduced stress, improved wellbeing, reduced depression.

People didn't become lazy. Some went back to school. Some started businesses. Some did volunteer work. Some just existed without constant stress for the first time.

Similar pilots in Canada, Kenya, India, United States found same results.

Give people enough money to meet basic needs without constant stress, and their mental health improves.

This isn't mysterious. This isn't complicated.

But it's politically impossible because acknowledging poverty causes depression would require acknowledging we've chosen to maintain systems that keep people poor.

The perverse economics

I met someone recently in Đà Lạt—another expat who'd fled crushing circumstances.

'I had everything wrong with me back in Sydney,' she said. 'Depression, anxiety, chronic fatigue. Seeing specialists, trying medications, nothing helped. Came here for holiday, felt better within a week. Eventually realised the problem wasn't me—it was trying to survive in a city where rent ate 80% of my income.'

'So you moved permanently?'

'Couldn't afford not to. Moving to Vietnam was cheaper than staying sick in Sydney.'

And that's the perverse economics: for some people, international relocation is more affordable than managing poverty-induced depression at home.

Let that percolate.

The bottom line

Here's what nobody tells you about poverty: it's not about not having luxury items or holidays.

It's the constant awareness you're one unexpected expense away from disaster.

It's standing in supermarket aisles calculating whether you can afford fruit.

It's lying awake at 3am worrying about appliances.

It's days without food because an unexpected bill ate your buffer.

It's wearing clothes that need replacing whilst owning a house worth hundreds of thousands on paper.

It's the cognitive load using 13 IQ points, leaving you stupider, more forgetful—then being judged for making bad decisions.

It's being told your entirely reasonable response to unreasonable circumstances is mental illness requiring pharmaceutical treatment.

And it's the shame of admitting any of this in a wealthy country where poverty is treated as moral failure.

Beyond the supermarket aisle

I want to be clear: I'm not arguing against medication or therapy. If you're depressed and medication helps, take it. If therapy gives you tools, use them.

But let's stop pretending individual treatment is sufficient when the problem is systemic.

Let's stop telling people their reasonable responses to poverty are brain diseases requiring lifelong medication rather than policy problems requiring political solutions.

Let's stop designing economic systems creating poverty at scale whilst maintaining fiction that anyone can succeed if they try hard enough.

And let's start asking whose interests are served by keeping poverty individualised and medicalised rather than recognised as systemic issue creating depression at rates far higher than random chance.

Because once we start asking those questions, we might have to change the systems.

And that would be terribly inconvenient.

Same income in different place. Everything changed.

Which raises rather uncomfortable question that nobody seems eager to explore: if my depression lifted when cost of living decreased whilst income remained constant, what does that say about the relationship between economics and mental health?

What does it say about the millions of people being medicated for reasonable responses to poverty?

But it wasn't just the money that changed when I moved to Vietnam. The pension going further was crucial—I'm not going to pretend otherwise, because poverty is real and material and affects everything.

But there was something else too. Something I didn't expect and didn't know how to name until I started reviewing my photography and realised my perception of reality had fundamentally shifted.

The world looked different here. Not metaphorically—literally different. I was seeing things I couldn't see in Adelaide even though they were presumably there.

Same eyes. Same camera. Completely different visual experience.

And that made me wonder: what if depression isn't just about systems and economics and neurodivergence, but also about something as simple and profound as whether your brain can function in the place where you're trying to exist?

References

Haushofer, J., & Fehr, E. (2014). On the psychology of poverty. *Science, 344*(6186), 862-867.

Mani, A., Mullainathan, S., Shafir, E., & Zhao, J. (2013). Poverty impedes cognitive function. *Science, 341*(6149), 976-980.

Richardson, T., Elliott, P., & Roberts, R. (2013). The relationship between personal unsecured debt and mental and physical health: A systematic review and meta-analysis. *Clinical Psychology Review, 33*(8), 1148-1162.

Sareen, J., Afifi, T. O., McMillan, K. A., & Asmundson, G. J. (2011). Relationship between household income and mental disorders: Findings from a population-based longitudinal study. *Archives of General Psychiatry, 68*(4), 419-427.

Chapter 5
The geography of mood

The photographic evidence

There's a photograph I took in Adelaide in early 2025, three months before I left.

It's a beach at dawn. Empty. Long exposure, so the water looks like fog. Sky various shades of grey that might charitably be called "atmospheric" or honestly described as "bleak as fuck."

A single piece of driftwood. Dramatic. Lonely. Beautiful in that way that makes people say "Wow, that's so moody" when what they mean is "Are you okay?"

I wasn't okay, as it happens.

Six months later in Vietnam, I'm photographing street vendors in Đà Lạt market. Full colour. Vibrant. A woman selling dragon fruit so red it looks oversaturated except it hasn't been Photoshopped. That's just what dragon fruit looks like when your nervous system isn't running at maximum capacity trying to survive.

Same camera. Same person. Same technical knowledge.

Completely different perception of reality.

Here's the thing: the world didn't change between Adelaide and Đà Lạt.

I did.

Or rather, my capacity to perceive the world changed because my environment changed in ways that reduced cognitive load required just to exist.

Which raises an uncomfortable question: if perception can shift this dramatically based on location, what does that say about the relationship between environment and mental health?

And more importantly: how many people are being treated for depression when what they actually need is a different postcode?

What Adelaide was like

Let me tell you what Adelaide was like in those final months.

Beautiful city, objectively. Gorgeous architecture. Excellent coffee culture. The sort of place that looks magnificent in tourism brochures.

For me, it was slowly crushing.

Not dramatically. Just the grinding daily reality of a city that cost more than my pension could cover. Every expense required calculation. The gap between what life cost and what I could afford created constant low-level anxiety.

The weather didn't help. Adelaide has particular quality of light in winter—grey, flat, like everything's been filmed through a dirty window. Summer was worse: forty-degree days where the sun beat down like punishment and air conditioning I couldn't afford to run became a source of guilt.

The sensory environment was exhausting. Constant traffic noise.

Sirens. Car alarms. The neighbour's dog that barked for hours. The couple next door who apparently moved furniture at 2am as a hobby.

The social expectations were worse. Australian tall poppy syndrome means you can't be too successful or too different. Casual cruelty disguised as "just joking, mate." The expectation that you'll care deeply about football and cricket.

The cultural assumption that if you're not coping, you're weak. That asking for help is failure. That being on pension marks you as lesser.

I didn't consciously recognise any of this.

I just knew getting through each day felt like wading through treacle whilst someone occasionally hit me with a stick.

My photography from that period tells the truth I couldn't articulate: everything was monochromatic, empty, isolating, slowly fading.

That wasn't artistic vision. That was my nervous system's honest perception of an environment hostile to my flourishing.

The evidence in the research

Here's what's weird about depression: we treat it as if it's happening inside your skull, independent of what's happening outside.

Brain chemistry. Neurotransmitters. Cognitive distortions. All very internal.

But what if depression is often your brain's accurate perception of your environment?

What if the problem isn't perceiving reality incorrectly, but that reality actually is threatening?

There's research on this. Studies on how environment affects mental health, how place shapes wellbeing.

A study in *Social Science & Medicine* tracked people who moved from high-stress to low-stress environments. Their cortisol dropped. Sleep improved. Self-reported wellbeing increased. Depression scores decreased.

Not because brains suddenly produced more serotonin. Because chronic environmental stressors were removed.

Another study in *Health & Place* examined how neighbourhood characteristics affect mental health. Not just poverty or crime—things like green space, community cohesion, walkability, noise levels, air quality.

Findings were remarkably consistent: people in environments with more green space, less noise, stronger community connections, cleaner air had significantly better mental health.

This isn't mysterious.

Humans evolved to thrive in certain environments. Natural settings with greenery. Relatively quiet spaces. Communities where we know neighbours. Clean air and water.

We didn't evolve to thrive in concrete cities with constant noise pollution, isolation, atomised social structures, air that tastes like car exhaust.

Some people cope fine. Their nervous systems are robust enough or circumstances privileged enough.

But some of us can't.

And when we can't, we're told the problem is our brains rather than our environments.

What Đà Lạt is like

Đà Lạt is nothing like Adelaide.

It's a small city in the Central Highlands. About 1,500 metres above sea level, which means temperature is mild year-round. None of

Adelaide's punishing summers or grey winters. Just pleasant. Consistently pleasant.

It's green. Spectacularly green. Pine trees everywhere. Gardens. Parks. The sort of lush vegetation that makes you remember humans are supposed to live around plants, not concrete.

It's relatively quiet. Scooters, certainly—this is Vietnam. But not the same aggressive urban cacophony. More gentle hum. White noise rather than assault.

The air is clean. Mountain air. You can breathe deeply without tasting pollution.

The social expectations are different in ways that accidentally suit my neurodivergent brain better. Vietnamese communication tends to be more direct than Australian. Less subtext to decode. Questions that would be rude in Australia are normal here. "How much do you pay for rent?" "How old are you?" "Are you married?" "Do you have a girlfriend?" Just questions, not invasions.

The pace is different. Less frantic. People aren't constantly rushing, constantly stressed.

And most importantly: my pension goes four times further here.

Four times.

Same money. Different purchasing power. Different possibilities.

The privilege narrative

I need to be clear about something: most people can't just move to another country when their environment is crushing them.

Most people don't have passports or pensions that travel or language skills or sheer bloody-minded willingness to start over at sixty-six in a place where you can't read street signs.

I'm not suggesting moving to Southeast Asia is a solution to depression. That would be absurd. The geographic equivalent of "just think positive."

What I am suggesting: if the same brain functions completely differently in different environments, maybe we should spend less time treating brains and more time examining environments.

Maybe we should ask: what is it about some places that crush people whilst other places allow flourishing?

Could we design environments that support human wellbeing instead of assuming anyone who can't cope with hostile environments has broken brain?

The expat community observation

Here's what I've noticed in the few months I've been here: it's not just me.

The expat community in Đà Lạt is full of people who've fled environments that were making them sick. Not all were depressed—some had anxiety, some had chronic pain that mysteriously improved, some just had vague sense they couldn't cope.

And most of them got better.

Not all. Vietnam isn't magic. But enough that it's noticeable.

We've started joking about it: "Đà Lạt, where broken people come to accidentally fix themselves."

Which raises the question: what is it about this place that works when other places don't?

Habitat mismatch

There's a concept in ecology called habitat mismatch.

When a species evolved for one environment finds itself in a different environment. The species isn't broken—it's just in wrong habitat.

A fish out of water isn't a broken fish. It's a perfectly good fish in an environment that can't support fish.

Put it back in water, and it's fine.

I wonder if depression works the same way sometimes.

Not always—some people have genuine neurological conditions requiring treatment regardless of environment.

But sometimes what looks like depression is just habitat mismatch. A perfectly good brain in an environment that can't support that particular brain.

The solution isn't fixing the brain. It's changing the habitat.

But that's deeply uncomfortable for modern society.

Because if we acknowledge environments matter more than brain chemistry, we'd have to acknowledge our cities and social structures and economic systems might be fundamentally hostile to human wellbeing.

We'd have to ask: why are depression rates skyrocketing in wealthy Western countries whilst remaining lower in poorer countries?

We'd have to examine: what are we doing wrong?

Much easier to say the problem is brain chemistry and prescribe medication.

The research on wealthy countries

A study in *The Lancet Psychiatry* compared depression rates across 30 countries.

Findings were fascinating and uncomfortable: depression rates were highest in wealthy Western countries. Places with advanced healthcare, high GDP, supposedly excellent quality of life.

Depression rates were lower in many poorer countries. Countries with significant poverty, political instability, limited healthcare.

This is opposite of what you'd expect if depression were primarily biological illness distributed randomly.

If depression were just brain chemistry, you'd expect similar rates everywhere, maybe slightly higher in countries with worse healthcare.

Instead, depression clusters in wealthy Western countries in ways suggesting our modern way of life might be the problem.

Researchers theorised several factors:

Social isolation in individualistic Western cultures versus community cohesion in collectivist cultures.

Pace of life—constant stress, competition, pressure to optimise versus more relaxed paces.

Disconnection from nature in urban Western environments versus more time outdoors.

Economic precarity despite wealth—constant awareness you're one job loss away from disaster versus acceptance of collective struggle.

Lack of meaning or purpose in modern Western life versus clearer roles and community contribution.

All environmental factors. All systemic issues. None fixed by medication alone.

The morning walk

I went for a walk this morning through Đà Lạt market, camera in hand.

Watched a woman selling vegetables arrange her produce—not just dumping it but creating little artistic displays. Watched children playing some complicated game involving a shuttlecock and their feet. Watched an elderly man practising tai chi whilst motorbikes and scooters whizzed past.

Normal life. Unremarkable moments.

But I could engage without feeling overwhelmed. Could photograph without exhaustion. Could be present without constant effort to manage nervous system.

Seven months ago in Adelaide, this would have been impossible.

Too much stimulation. Too many people. I'd have lasted twenty minutes before needing to retreat.

Here, it's just a morning walk, followed by a coffee in a café. (Side-note: coffee in Đà Lạt is the equivalent of limoncello in Italy; stunningly tasty, utterly more-ish, totally ubiquitous).

Nothing special. Nothing requiring heroic effort.

Just existing in the world like a regular human.

That's the difference between environment that suits you and one that doesn't.

The unanswered question

I need to be honest: I don't know if my recovery is about Vietnam specifically or just about "not Adelaide."

Could I have achieved same results by moving to Tasmania? Rural Queensland? Bloody Perth?

I don't know.

I chose Vietnam partly because of cost of living. Partly because I'd visited Southeast Asia before and loved it. Partly because at sixty-six, starting over somewhere completely foreign felt like either brilliant adventure or catastrophically stupid decision, and I was too exhausted to care which.

It worked.

But I can't tell you if it worked because Vietnam is special or because anywhere different would have been better than where I was.

Maybe the improvement is just about escaping environment that was crushing me. Maybe any change would have helped.

Or maybe there's something specific about this place—the altitude, the climate, the culture, the people, the pace—that suits my particular neurology.

I genuinely don't know.

What I know with certainty: the same brain that couldn't function in Adelaide is functioning fine here.

Environment changed. Brain didn't.

Outcomes changed completely.

Which suggests maybe the problem was never primarily about my brain.

The uncomfortable implication

Here's what makes me uncomfortable about my own recovery: it required extraordinary privilege.

Age privilege—nothing tying me to Australia. Pension privilege—income that travels. Property privilege—house to sell. Passport privilege—Australian passport opens doors. Education privilege—understanding how to research and navigate bureaucracy. Health privilege—reasonably healthy at sixty-six.

Side note: It came as a shock to me that on my first visit for a medical checkup here in Đà Lạt, the results came back that I was perfectly healthy. Nothing that would cause any medical practitioner the slightest bit of worry. I had assumed that all the tablets I had been taking for decades for various physical conditions were necessary; it turns out they weren't. And it wasn't 'third world' technology that had assessed me—this was state of the art technology, the results of which were assessed by highly trained practitioners. The medical system here in Vietnam—at least in the private sector—is better than the medical system in Australia, imho.

Back to my privileges…

Most people don't have these privileges. Most people can't escape crushing environments no matter how much those environments are harming them.

Which means my recovery, whilst real, doesn't solve anything systemic.

Individual escape only works for individuals with sufficient privilege.

Everyone else remains trapped in environments making them sick, being told the problem is their brains rather than their circumstances.

And celebrating individual escapes whilst ignoring systemic problems just reinforces the idea that anyone who remains trapped isn't trying hard enough.

The cultural dimension

But there's something else I've noticed here, something harder to quantify.

Vietnamese culture makes more sense to me than Australian culture ever did.

The social expectations are different. The pace is different. The way people interact is different.

I fit here in ways I never quite fit back home.

Though I spent sixty-six years assuming the problem was me rather than the fit between me and my environment.

And that raises another question: what if some depression is cultural mismatch rather than just environmental stress?

What if some people's brains simply don't align with the culture they're born into?

My depression lifted when I moved from Adelaide to Đà Lạt. Same brain, different place, completely different mental health.

Which proves... what, exactly?

That geography determines mental health? That everyone should move to Vietnam? That I got lucky and found a place that happened to suit my particular neurology through pure chance?

I don't know.

What I do know is that place matters more than we acknowledge. Environment shapes perception. Circumstances determine outcomes more than mindset ever will.

But there's another dimension to environment that I haven't fully addressed yet. One that's been lurking throughout this entire book, implicit in every story about not fitting, about exhausting social performances, about feeling perpetually wrong.

It's not just about physical environment—weather and green space and noise levels and cost of living, though those matter enormously.

It's also about cultural environment. About the unwritten rules that govern what's acceptable and what's pathological. About who gets to define "normal" and what happens to everyone who falls outside that definition.

In my life so far I have spent twenty-two years in British culture, and forty-four years in Australian culture, feeling like I was constantly getting it wrong without understanding what "it" was. Then I moved to Vietnamese and suddenly I wasn't getting it wrong anymore.

Same brain. Different culture. Different rules about what counts as acceptable human behaviour.

And that raises questions about how much of what we call "mental illness" is actually just cultural mismatch—people whose brains don't align with the culture they're born into, being told the problem is their brains rather than the misalignment.

References

Gascon, M., Triguero-Mas, M., Martínez, D., Dadvand, P., Forns, J., Plasència, A., & Nieuwenhuijsen, M. J. (2015). Mental health benefits of long-term exposure to residential green and blue spaces: A systematic review. *International Journal of Environmental Research and Public Health, 12*(4), 4354-4379.

Hartig, T., Mitchell, R., De Vries, S., & Frumkin, H. (2014). Nature and health. *Annual Review of Public Health, 35*, 207-228.

Lund, C., Breen, A., Flisher, A. J., Kakuma, R., Corrigall, J., Joska, J. A., Swartz, L., & Patel, V. (2010). Poverty and common mental disorders in low and middle income countries: A systematic review. *Social Science & Medicine, 71*(3), 517-528.

Maas, J., Verheij, R. A., de Vries, S., Spreeuwenberg, P., Schellevis, F. G., & Groenewegen, P. P. (2009). Morbidity is related to a green living environment. *Journal of Epidemiology & Community Health, 63*(12), 967-973.

World Health Organization. (2017). *Depression and other common mental disorders: Global health estimates.* Geneva: World Health Organization.

Chapter 6
Cultural mismatch

The barbecue transgression

I once attended a barbecue in Adelaide where I committed the cardinal sin of Australian social interaction: I answered a question honestly.

'How's things, mate?' someone asked whilst handing me a beer.

'Not great, actually,' I said. 'Been struggling a bit. Finances are tight, the house needs repairs I can't afford, and I'm having trouble sleeping because—'

The look on his face stopped me mid-sentence.

Part confusion, part discomfort, part "why are you making this weird by being honest?"

'Yeah, righto,' he said, backing away slowly. 'Well, she'll be right, mate. She'll be right.'

End of conversation.

I stood there holding my beer, realising I'd just violated the fundamental Australian cultural contract: you're supposed to say you're fine. Always fine.

Being actually not fine is un-Australian.

Rather like admitting you don't care about cricket or think Vegemite is overrated.

This is what I mean when I talk about cultural mismatch.

Tall poppy syndrome explained

Australian culture has some brilliant features, genuinely.

The larrikin spirit. Irreverence towards authority. The egalitarian streak that says nobody's better than anyone else.

But it also has features that are considerably less brilliant if you don't fit the mould.

Tall poppy syndrome, for instance.

For the uninitiated: tall poppy syndrome is the cultural tendency to cut down anyone who gets too successful, too accomplished, too obviously better than everyone else.

Sounds reasonable in theory—nobody should think they're better. In practice, it means you can't be too successful without people resenting you. Can't be too smart without people thinking you're up yourself. Can't be too different without being told you're not quite Australian enough.

And you definitely can't admit you're struggling without people suggesting you're weak.

It's culture that values conformity whilst pretending to value individualism. Values toughness whilst pretending to value mateship. Values silence about suffering whilst pretending to value honest communication.

The cognitive dissonance is exhausting even before you add neurodivergence.

"She'll be right" as dismissive weapon

Let me tell you about "she'll be right," possibly the most Australian phrase ever devised and possibly the most psychologically damaging.

"She'll be right" means: don't worry, it'll work out, no point stressing.

It's meant to be reassuring. Optimistic.

In practice, it's dismissing problems without addressing them.

Your house is falling apart? She'll be right.

You can't afford food? She'll be right.

You're depressed and suicidal? She'll be right, mate, just have a beer and watch the footy.

It's particularly brutal when combined with cultural prohibition against admitting you're not fine. You're struggling, you finally work up courage to mention it, and someone responds with "she'll be right" as if optimism is solution to material circumstances.

Like being told to think positively about drowning.

The worst part: "she'll be right" contains implicit criticism. If you're still worried after being told she'll be right, you're the problem. You're not tough enough. Not Australian enough.

So you learn to shut up, bottle up concerns, pretend everything's fine even when it's manifestly not.

And then wonder why you're depressed.

Mateship with rules

Australian mateship—the idea that mates look after mates—is genuinely beautiful in theory.

In practice, mateship has rules.

You can rely on mates for help moving house or lending tools or showing up when your car breaks down. Practical help, material support.

But you can't rely on mates for emotional support without making it weird.

Can't admit you're depressed without worrying they'll think you're weak. Can't ask for help with mental health without violating unspoken rule that real blokes don't have feelings requiring discussion. That's wimm'n work.

So mateship becomes this strange performance where you're simultaneously part of community and completely isolated within it.

You can have a dozen mates who'd help you move furniture but not one person you can tell you're thinking about killing yourself.

That's not mateship. That's organised furniture moving with beer.

Australian communication as foreign language

The communication style in Australian culture is interesting if you're neurodivergent, by which I mean "exhausting and confusing and like learning a foreign language that everyone insists isn't actually a language."

Australians communicate indirectly.

We don't say what we mean. We imply it. We suggest it. We leave massive gaps between what's said and what's meant, and you're expected to intuitively understand subtext.

"We should grab a coffee sometime" doesn't mean "let's schedule coffee." It means "I'm being polite but have no actual intention of seeing you."

"That's interesting" doesn't mean "that's interesting." It means "I disagree but I'm too polite to say so directly."

"No worries" doesn't always mean "no worries." Sometimes it means "actually there are worries but I'm performing easy-going."

For neurotypical Australians, this is apparently intuitive.

For neurodivergent Australians, it's a nightmare.

I spent decades trying to decode Australian communication. Learning unspoken rules. Memorising scripts. Analysing interactions afterwards to figure out where I'd misunderstood subtext.

It's exhausting.

And when you don't understand subtext, people think you're being deliberately obtuse or rude. They can't conceive you genuinely don't know what they meant, because to them the meaning is obvious.

You're constantly getting interactions wrong whilst having no idea what you've done wrong because nobody will tell you directly—that would be rude.

It's like playing a game where everyone knows the rules except you, and when you ask what the rules are, people look at you like you're insane.

Vietnamese culture differences

Vietnamese culture is different.

Not better necessarily—just different in ways that happen to work better for my particular neurological configuration.

Vietnamese communication tends to be more direct. People say what they mean. If they want to know something, they ask. If they disagree, they say so.

This was disorienting at first. Someone asked how much I paid for rent within five minutes of meeting me, and I nearly had a cultural heart attack.

Here, it's normal. They're curious. They want information. So they ask.

Revolutionary concept: wanting information and asking for it directly.

Similarly, if someone doesn't want to do something, they say no. Not "maybe," not "I'll see," not "that sounds interesting" whilst having no intention. Just "no."

For a neurodivergent brain that struggles with reading subtext, this is like suddenly being able to breathe after years holding your breath underwater.

I don't have to decode what people mean. They say what they mean.

Communication becomes straightforward exchange of information rather than elaborate dance of implication.

The cognitive load reduction is extraordinary.

Cultural fit and mental health research

Here's something interesting about culture and mental health: culture determines what counts as "normal" and what counts as "pathological."

In Australia, if you need lots of downtime after social interactions, you're antisocial. If you don't intuitively understand subtext, you're socially incompetent. If you can't handle open-plan offices, you're difficult.

The problem is you.

In Vietnam, needing downtime is just needing downtime. Not understanding subtext is fine because there's less subtext. Not liking open-plan environments is understandable—they're loud and chaotic.

You're just a person who exists in ways that happen to fit better here.

Same brain. Same behaviours. Different cultural context.

In Australia, pathological. In Vietnam, normal.

Which raises uncomfortable question: how much of what we call "mental illness" is actually just cultural mismatch?

The tall poppy syndrome and business failures

The tall poppy syndrome had interesting effects on my businesses.

In Australia, if your business succeeds too much, people resent you. If you talk about success, you're up yourself. If you market yourself effectively, you're a wanker.

The cultural expectation is that you should be successful but not too successful, and definitely not talk about it.

This creates bizarre dynamic where you're supposed to run a business —which requires self-promotion and marketing—whilst also pretending you're not really trying that hard because trying hard is uncool.

I internalised this thoroughly. Undersold my skills. Apologised for charging money. Downplayed my qualifications because talking about them seemed arrogant.

My research had been cited over 1,200 times. That's genuinely impressive. But mentioning it felt like bragging, so I didn't.

In Vietnam, nobody cares about tall poppies. If you're good at something, people want to know. If you have qualifications, they're interested.

Self-promotion isn't arrogance—it's providing information.

It's like someone removed a weight I didn't know I was carrying.

I wonder how many Australian businesses fail not because owners lack skills but because tall poppy syndrome makes effective self-promotion feel culturally transgressive.

Person-environment fit

There's a concept in psychology called "person-environment fit."

How well a person fits their environment.

High fit means your characteristics align with environmental demands. You thrive. Everything feels natural.

Low fit means constant friction. Everything requires more effort than it should. You're swimming upstream whilst everyone else floats downstream.

I had low person-environment fit in Australia.

Not because Australia is bad—it's perfectly good culture for people whose neurology aligns with Australian cultural values.

But I'm neurodivergent, introverted and at the same time socially skilled at public speaking, direct in communication, not interested in sports, terrible at decoding subtext.

Every social interaction required more effort than it should have. Every workplace was designed for neurotypical extroverts. Every cultural expectation rubbed against my natural inclinations.

Like wearing shoes that don't quite fit. Not painful enough to be unbearable, but uncomfortable enough that you're always aware of them.

After decades of ill-fitting shoes, your feet start to hurt in ways you assume are just how feet feel.

Until you try shoes that fit, and suddenly realise: oh, feet aren't supposed to hurt constantly. That was just the shoes.

Vietnam is shoes that fit.

Not perfect—nowhere is perfect. But shoes that fit well enough that I'm not constantly aware of friction between who I am and what's expected.

Code-switching exhaustion

Let me tell you about the exhaustion of code-switching between cultures.

Code-switching is when you change behaviour and language to fit different social contexts. Everyone does it to some degree.

But cross-cultural code-switching is more demanding.

When I talk to Australian friends, I have to remember: don't be too direct, decode the subtext, use right amount of irony, downplay success, definitely don't talk about feelings, maintain performance of being fine.

When I talk to Vietnamese friends, I can just talk. Say what I mean. Ask direct questions. Answer honestly.

The difference in cognitive load is remarkable.

After video call with Australian friends, I need recovery time. Feel exhausted.

After coffee with Vietnamese friends, I just move on with my day. No recovery needed. Because I wasn't performing, I was just existing.

This is what cultural fit means practically: whether existing in a culture requires constant performance or whether you can just be.

The specific tiredness

I need to acknowledge something: I'm not saying Vietnamese culture is objectively better than Australian culture.

I'm saying Vietnamese culture happens to fit my neurology better.

For neurotypical extroverts who thrive on mateship and love sports and intuitively understand Australian communication, Australia is probably brilliant.

For neurodivergent introverts who prefer direct communication and don't care about sports and find tall poppy syndrome exhausting, Australia is harder.

Neither culture is better. They're just designed for different types of humans.

The problem is cultures don't acknowledge this. Instead, they treat their particular way of being human as the only correct way, and pathologise everyone who doesn't fit.

In Australia, if you don't fit Australian cultural norms, you're the problem. You need to try harder. Be more social. Care more about sports. Learn to decode subtext. Toughen up. Be more Australian.

The idea that maybe Australian culture isn't designed for all types of humans—that's not part of the conversation.

So people spend decades thinking they're broken when actually they're just in wrong culture for their neurology.

What happened to my mental health

Here's what happened to my mental health when I moved from culture that didn't fit to one that did:

The anxiety I'd assumed was intrinsic to my personality largely disappeared.

Turns out it wasn't anxiety disorder. It was entirely reasonable response to constantly navigating cultural environment that didn't make intuitive sense.

The social exhaustion I'd thought was introversion requiring careful management disappeared too.

Turns out I'm not that introverted. I was just exhausted from constant cultural code-switching and performing neurotypicality.

The depression lifted—we've covered that. But what I didn't expect was how much of my depression had been tied to cultural mismatch.

Not all of it. The poverty was real, the systemic betrayal was real, the neurodivergent masking exhaustion was real.

But the constant feeling of being wrong, of not fitting, of failing at basic human interaction—that lifted when culture changed.

Same brain. Different cultural context. Completely different mental health outcomes.

The research on culture and mental health

There's research on this—culture and mental health, how cultural contexts affect what behaviours get labelled pathological.

A study in *Culture, Medicine, and Psychiatry* found that behaviours considered disordered in one culture were considered normal in another.

What counts as "too emotional" or "too withdrawn" or "too direct" varies dramatically across cultures.

Another study in *Transcultural Psychiatry* examined how individualist versus collectivist cultures shaped depression presentation. In individualist cultures like Australia, depression was seen as individual pathology. In collectivist cultures, similar symptoms were understood as reasonable responses to social circumstances.

A review in *Annual Review of Clinical Psychology* found diagnostic rates for mental illnesses varied dramatically across cultures—not because some cultures had more mental illness, but because cultures defined pathology differently.

What counts as mental illness is partly cultural construct.

Not entirely—some neurological conditions exist regardless of cultural context. But the line between "different" and "disordered" is drawn differently depending on what a culture values.

The bottom line

Here's what I wonder about culture and mental health:

What if we acknowledged that cultures are designed for particular types of humans, and not all humans fit all cultures?

What if we stopped treating cultural mismatch as individual pathology?

What if we expanded definitions of acceptable behaviour to include more neurotypes, more personality types, more ways of being human?

What if we designed workplaces accommodating both introverts and extroverts, neurotypical and neurodivergent brains, direct and indirect communicators?

I'm not suggesting everyone should move to cultures that fit better—that's obviously not practical.

But I am suggesting we should stop assuming people who don't fit their culture are broken and need fixing.

Maybe they're fine. Maybe the culture's definition of acceptable behaviour is too narrow.

Maybe we need more acceptance of difference.

Because treating cultural mismatch as mental illness isn't helping anyone except pharmaceutical companies and therapists who benefit from medicalising reasonable response to cultural environments hostile to particular neurotypes.

When systems become the enemy

I spent decades trying to fit Australian cultural definitions.

Trying to be more extroverted, more interested in sports, better at decoding subtext, tougher about problems, less emotionally open.

It didn't work. Just made me exhausted and depressed and convinced something was fundamentally wrong with me.

Moving to Vietnam didn't fix everything—I still have the same brain, same neurodivergence, same history.

But it removed constant friction of cultural mismatch.

And that made all the difference.

Same brain. Different culture. Different outcomes.

Maybe that's not about brain chemistry at all.

Maybe it's about cultural fit.

So I was neurodivergent in a neurotypical culture, poor in an expensive city, crushed by systems designed to fail me, and my brain couldn't function in the environment where I was trying to exist.

No wonder I was depressed.

The real question: what could I actually do about any of it?

Because here's the deeply uncomfortable truth that's been lurking throughout this entire book: I escaped. Through extraordinary privilege and luck and stubbornness, I managed to change my circumstances in ways that most people can't.

I moved to another country. Started over at sixty-six. Found environment and culture that suited my neurology better. Discovered my pension could cover comfortable living if I just lived somewhere else.

And my depression lifted.

But that solution—"just move to Vietnam"—is spectacularly unhelpful for the vast majority of people reading this book. Most people can't relocate internationally. Can't leave jobs they need. Can't abandon dependents. Can't afford the risk even if they have the resources.

So what's the point of telling my story if it's not generalisable? If my solution only works for people with my particular constellation of privileges?

That's the question I've been wrestling with since my depression lifted. Because individual escape stories can either inspire genuine change or they can become bootstraps mythology—proof that anyone who remains trapped just isn't trying hard enough.

Let me tell you what individual change actually looks like when international relocation isn't an option. What you can do when you can't escape but need to survive anyway.

And more importantly: let me tell you why individual solutions, whilst valid and valuable, are never sufficient when the problem is systemic.

References

Heine, S. J., & Lehman, D. R. (1995). Cultural variation in unrealistic optimism: Does the West feel more vulnerable than the East? *Journal of Personality and Social Psychology, 68*(4), 595-607.

Hofstede, G. (2011). Dimensionalizing cultures: The Hofstede model in context. *Online Readings in Psychology and Culture, 2*(1), 1-26.

Kirmayer, L. J. (2001). Cultural variations in the clinical presentation of depression and anxiety: Implications for diagnosis and treatment. *Journal of Clinical Psychiatry, 62*(13), 22-30.

Kleinman, A. (2004). Culture and depression. *New England Journal of Medicine, 351*(10), 951-953.

Markus, H. R., & Kitayama, S. (1991). Culture and the self: Implications for cognition, emotion, and motivation. *Psychological Review, 98*(2), 224-253.

Ryder, A. G., Yang, J., Zhu, X., Yao, S., Yi, J., Heine, S. J., & Bagby, R. M. (2008). The cultural shaping of depression: Somatic symptoms in China, psychological symptoms in North America? *Journal of Abnormal Psychology, 117*(2), 300-313.

Chapter 7
Individual change when possible

The 3am decision

I made the decision to move to Vietnam whilst sitting in my Gawler house at 3am, unable to sleep because the hot water system was making ominous noises again.

This is not how sensible life decisions are supposed to be made.

Sensible life decisions involve research, planning, pros-and-cons lists, consultation with trusted advisors. Possibly a vision board if you're into that sort of thing.

My decision involved sitting in the dark at 3am thinking: "Fuck this."

I'm sixty-six years old. I've served my country. I've earned degrees that people still cite. I've published research contributing to the field. And I'm lying awake worrying about hot water systems I can't afford to replace in a house slowly falling apart around me in a city where my pension doesn't cover basic survival.

There has to be somewhere else that makes more sense than this.

Then I googled "cheap places to live on Australian pension" like some sort of geriatric digital nomad researching escape routes.

Vietnam came up repeatedly. Forums full of expats saying the same thing: Australian pension goes much further, cost of living is reasonable, healthcare is affordable, food is excellent.

But here's the thing: Vietnam wasn't random.

I'd been to Southeast Asia before. Lived in Penang, Malaysia, during my RAAF service. Years ago now, different life.

But something about that time had stuck. The freedom outside the base. Mingling with people from various Southeast Asian countries who seemed genuinely happy despite having what looked like poverty by Western standards.

That had confused me then. How could people with so little be so content?

I didn't understand what I was observing. Just knew something about Southeast Asia felt right in ways Australia never quite had.

So when Vietnam came up at 3am, it wasn't just practical calculation. It was something deeper.

Let's talk about privilege

Let's be absolutely clear about something: my entire "just move to Vietnam" story requires enormous privilege most people don't have.

I had privilege in multiple forms:

Age privilege: At sixty-six, nothing tied me to Australia. No job to leave. No dependent children. No caregiving responsibilities. Nobody relying on me to stay put.

Pension privilege: Guaranteed income that travels internationally. Most people's income is tied to location through employment.

Property privilege: I owned a house I could sell. Had equity. Had something to convert into moving costs even though proceeds were tiny after mortgage and debts.

Passport privilege: Australian passport gets you into most countries relatively easily. Visa options unavailable to people from many other countries.

Education privilege: I speak English fluently, have advanced qualifications, understand how bureaucratic systems work, know how to research and evaluate information.

Health privilege: At sixty-six, reasonably healthy. No conditions requiring specialised treatment only available in Australia.

Neurodivergence privilege: My particular brand of AuDHD makes change easier rather than harder for me specifically. For many neurodivergent people, change is traumatic. For me, it was energising.

So when I say "individual change when possible," I'm acutely aware that "possible" is doing enormous work in that sentence.

For me, it was possible because of accumulated privilege I didn't necessarily earn but definitely benefited from.

For most people, it's not possible.

Not because they're not trying hard enough. Because they don't have the specific constellation of privileges required.

The house sale

I sold the Gawler house in October 2024.

The house selling process is excruciating. Firstly, selling my house in Athelstone; that house represented decades of history—my mother's house, where I'd lived whilst she was alive, her things, her memories.

Selling it felt like betrayal even though she was dead and definitely didn't care.

But I couldn't afford to maintain it. Couldn't afford to keep living in it. Couldn't afford the constant awareness it was slowly falling apart.

So I sold it.

Moved to Gawler. A moment of clarity in a Bunnings carpark meant that I'd have to sell my house sooner or later anyway… either to continue living in Australia but in my car, or move to somewhere where I could afford to breath.

Real estate agents wanted to "stage" it with furniture I didn't have and optimism I couldn't afford. Potential buyers wandered through commenting on everything wrong with it.

Sold for less than I'd hoped but more than I'd feared. The proceeds, after paying off mortgage and debts, were tiny.

Not "starting a new life" money. More like "surviving the first few months whilst figuring things out" money.

But tiny is more than nothing.

And nothing is what most people have.

May 2, 2025

May 2, 2025. Sydney to Ho Chi Minh City on one-way ticket.

I'd spent previous months researching obsessively. Reading expat forums, joining Facebook groups, asking approximately five thousand questions about everything from visa requirements to whether my camera equipment would survive tropical humidity.

The obsessive research was partly practical necessity and partly neuro-divergent hyperfocus finding something useful to fixate on.

Arrived in HCMC. Humid. Hot. The sort of tropical assault that makes you reconsider life choices within minutes.

Then waited three and a half hours for connection to Đà Lạt.

Three and a half hours in heat that felt like being slowly cooked. Questioned my decisions. Questioned my sanity. Questioned whether this was actually good idea or just expensive midlife crisis at sixty-six.

Then I landed at Liên Khương Airport—the proper name for Đà Lạt's airport, though nobody calls it that.

Stepped off the plane.

Smelled the air.

And knew I was home.

Landing at Liên Khương Airport

This sounds like inspirational travel memoir territory. "I knew immediately this was where I belonged." "The universe was calling me."

Except it actually happened.

The air smelled different. Not just fresh—mountain fresh. Clean. But also somehow familiar.

Then I realised: Penang.

It smelled like Penang had smelled forty-odd years ago when I was stationed there with the RAAF.

That same combination of mountain air and tropical greenery and something ineffable that probably isn't actually in the air but in my brain's response to it.

Standing outside the airport, I felt the same thing I'd felt in Penang: excitement mixed with adventure mixed with sense of being at one with a place despite being obviously foreign.

In Penang, I'd been depressed beyond belief with the military system. But outside the base, mingling with people from various Southeast Asian countries—that had felt right.

Forty years later, smelling that same air, I made a decision: this is where I'm laying down roots for the last time.

This is where I'll stay until I die.

It was immediate. Absolute. The sort of certainty I rarely experience.

But this was certain.

I was home.

The CX-5 as survival equipment

I took my tiny house sale proceeds and did something that probably looked insane: bought a brand new Mazda CX-5.

My third CX-5, actually. I know what I like.

This probably requires explanation because it sounds like terrible financial planning.

But here's the thing: driving isn't just transport for me. It's therapy. It's meditation. It's how I recharge when my internal battery runs flat.

I've loved driving since I got my license at sixteen. Not the going-somewhere part—the driving itself. Long distances at night became my lifeblood, my escape from a world I couldn't navigate.

Put me in social situations and I'm exhausted within hours. Put me in a car for eight hours with music and audiobooks and I emerge energised.

This isn't frivolous. This is essential infrastructure for my neurology.

So yes, I bought an expensive car with tiny proceeds from selling my house. Because I knew I'd need that infrastructure in Vietnam as much as I'd needed it in Australia.

The CX-5 wasn't luxury. It is survival equipment.

What individual change actually looked like

Let's talk about what individual change looked like practically, because "I knew I was home" is lovely but doesn't pay the rent.

First few weeks: Tourist visa, hotel, exploring. Getting feel for the city beyond airport sensory impressions. Walking neighbourhoods. Visiting markets. Figuring out if immediate sense of rightness would survive actually living here.

It survived.

Finding housing: Rented apartment in quiet neighbourhood—not the expat area where everyone speaks English and recreates Australia with cheaper beer. Wanted to actually live in Vietnam.

Rent was $400 per month for nice one-bedroom apartment with a breathtaking view from my balcony. In Adelaide, that wouldn't have covered a room in a share house with questionable plumbing.

Sorting the visa: Tourist visas are fine for visiting but inadequate for living. Needed something more stable. Found immigration lawyer who sorted out temporary residence card.

Process required approximately seventeen thousand documents, all apostilled and translated, but the lawyer handled it and it was remarkably straightforward by bureaucratic standards.

Building routine: This is where the CX-5 became essential. Started driving. Exploring. Learning roads. Taking long drives up mountains, down mountains, around lakes, through pine forests.

People thought I was mad. "You moved to Vietnam to drive around by yourself?"

Yes. Exactly. That's precisely what I needed.

Driving recharged my battery. Gave me processing time. Let me exist without performing social interaction.

Photography: Started shooting again. Really shooting. The vibrant colours, the street life, the markets, the people—everything I'd struggled to see in Adelaide suddenly visible.

Social connections: This happened gradually, organically. Met other expats at cafes. Joined photography groups. Started chatting with local vendors.

Nothing forced, nothing scheduled. Just natural accumulation of low-key connections.

The key: I could be myself. Being foreign excused social oddities. Being direct wasn't rude. Needing recovery time wasn't antisocial.

Healthcare: Registered with local clinic. Found doctors who spoke adequate English. Discovered healthcare here is both better and cheaper than Australia.

All of this was possible because I had pension that travels, small financial buffer, no dependents, health good enough to relocate, skills to navigate bureaucracy, language skills, neurology that found change energising.

Remove any of those factors and the whole thing becomes impossible.

The transformation timeline

Here's what individual change looked like for my mental health:

Week one: Still depressed but optimistic-depressed. The sort that says "I feel terrible but maybe this will work" rather than "I feel terrible and this is permanent."

Week three: Starting to notice things. Sleeping better. Constant background anxiety about money had diminished.

Week six: Realising I'd gone entire day without calculating disaster scenarios. When did that happen?

Week eight: Photography had shifted. Reviewing recent work and noticing: colour. Vibrancy. People. Life.

Two months: The depression had lifted. Not gradually—somewhere between week six and week eight, the crushing weight just wasn't there anymore.

Not because I'd found right medication. Not because I'd had therapeutic breakthrough.

Because circumstances creating and maintaining my depression no longer existed.

Financial stress? Reduced dramatically.

Cultural mismatch? Eliminated.

Sensory overwhelm? Manageable.

Masking exhaustion? Reduced.

Social isolation? Improved.

Same brain. Same neurotransmitters. Different circumstances.

Depression gone.

What individual change looks like when you can't move countries

Because I'm acutely aware my story is interesting but not generalisable.

Most people can't move to Vietnam. Can't sell houses they don't own. Can't leave jobs they need. Can't abandon dependents. Can't navigate international bureaucracy.

So what can individual change mean when your circumstances are largely unchangeable?

Here's what I learned:

Identify what specifically is crushing you: Not "everything" but specific things. Job? Housing? Location? Social environment? Financial situation?

You can't change everything. But you might be able to change something.

Distinguish between what you can change and what you can't: Some things are genuinely unchangeable. But some things are changeable with resources and planning.

Focus energy on changeable things: Don't waste resources on things you can't change. Accept they're shit. Then put energy toward things you can influence.

Recognise small changes accumulate: You can't overhaul your life overnight. But can you change one thing this month? Another next month?

Maybe you can't move cities, but can you move neighbourhoods? Can't change jobs but can you negotiate one day working from home? Can't eliminate financial stress but can you join community garden to reduce food costs?

Small changes won't cure depression caused by massive systemic problems. But they might create enough breathing room to survive whilst advocating for bigger changes.

Use whatever privileges you have: If you have any advantages—education, language skills, internet access, social support, stable housing—use them strategically.

Privilege isn't all-or-nothing. You can lack significant privileges whilst having some advantages you can leverage.

Here's what I'm absolutely not saying

"Just move to Southeast Asia!" Too expensive, too difficult, requires too much privilege.

"Just change your circumstances!" If people could just change crushing circumstances, they would.

"If I could do it, anyone can!" I had specific advantages most people lack.

"Geography determines mental health!" I got lucky that Vietnam suited my neurology. For someone else, Vietnam might be worse.

What I am saying:

Sometimes the problem really is circumstances, not brain. If you can identify what circumstances are crushing you—and if you have resources and privileges to change them—changing them might work better than endlessly treating symptoms.

For me, changeable circumstances included: geographic location, cultural environment, cost of living, sensory environment, social expectations.

For you, changeable circumstances might be different. Job. Relationship. Housing. Social environment. Daily routine.

The point isn't everyone should move to Vietnam.

The point is we should stop assuming depression is always primarily about brain chemistry when often it's primarily about circumstances.

I don't know if this will last

I need to be honest: I don't know if my recovery will last.

Four months is not very long. Depression could return. Circumstances could change. Vietnam could stop working.

Maybe this is honeymoon phase. Maybe I'll be writing different chapter in a year about how it fell apart.

I don't know.

What I know: for first time in decades, I'm not depressed. I'm sleeping, as much as my night-owl brain and years of shiftwork in the military allow. I'm taking photographs that don't look like visual representations of despair.

My brain is functioning better than it has in years—not because brain changed, but because circumstances changed.

That might not last. But it's lasted four months longer than any medication managed.

I'm cautiously optimistic. Which itself is remarkable, because optimism hasn't been part of my emotional repertoire for decades.

The bottom line on individual change

I'm not claiming I've found solution to depression.

I'm offering one data point: sometimes changing circumstances works when changing brain chemistry doesn't.

And if you have extraordinary privilege of being able to change your circumstances, it might be worth trying.

Even if it means moving to another country at sixty-six and buying an expensive car so you can drive around mountain roads listening to 80s synth-pop and ambient music whilst your brain slowly remembers how to not be crushed.

But individual escape doesn't fix systems

Here's what bothers me: the fact that I escaped doesn't mean the system is fine.

Every time someone escapes crushing circumstances through individual effort, people use it as evidence the system works brilliantly and everyone else just needs to try harder.

"See? He made it out. If you just try hard enough, you can too."

Which is bollocks.

I escaped because I had specific privileges most people lack. Remove any of those factors and I'd still be in Gawler, lying awake worrying about hot water systems.

Individual solutions only work for individuals who have required privileges.

Systemic solutions work for everyone.

And celebrating individual escapes whilst ignoring systemic problems just means systems never change whilst individuals with sufficient privilege escape and everyone else remains trapped.

So yes, change your circumstances if you can.

But also: advocate for systemic change so fewer people need to escape because systems work better for more people.

Both/and. Not either/or.

Individual change when possible. Systemic change always.

I escaped. Through privilege. Through luck. Through specific circumstances most people don't have and never will.

And I'm cautiously optimistic that my escape will last, though I'm honest enough to admit I don't know for certain.

But here's what bothers me about my own story: every time someone escapes crushing circumstances through individual effort, it's used as evidence that the systems are fine and everyone else just needs to try harder.

"See? He made it out. Just work harder. Be more resilient. Manifest abundance. Buy my course on entrepreneurial mindset."

Bollocks.

My escape proves the opposite. It proves the systems are broken. Proves that identical income produces completely different outcomes depending on where you exist. Proves that same brain functions differently in different environments. Proves that we could design better systems but choose not to.

Individual escape is valid. If you can change your circumstances, change them. No guilt. No shame. Survive however you can.

But individual escape doesn't fix systems. It just means one person got lucky whilst millions remain trapped.

And celebrating individual escapes whilst ignoring systemic problems is how systems perpetuate themselves indefinitely—by convincing everyone that escape is possible through individual effort whilst maintaining crushing circumstances that make escape available only to people with sufficient privilege.

So yes, change your circumstances if you can.

But also—and this is crucial—never stop advocating for systemic change so fewer people need to escape in the first place.

Because resilience is what we celebrate when we refuse to fix systems. And I'm tired of being called resilient when I should never have needed to be.

References

Berry, J. W. (1997). Immigration, acculturation, and adaptation. *Applied Psychology, 46*(1), 5-34.

Bhugra, D., & Becker, M. A. (2005). Migration, cultural bereavement and cultural identity. *World Psychiatry, 4*(1), 18-24.

Oishi, S., & Graham, J. (2010). Social ecology: Lost and found in psychological science. *Perspectives on Psychological Science, 5*(4), 356-377.

Ryff, C. D., & Keyes, C. L. M. (1995). The structure of psychological well-being revisited. *Journal of Personality and Social Psychology, 69*(4), 719-729.

Ward, C., Bochner, S., & Furnham, A. (2001). *The psychology of culture shock* (2nd ed.). Hove: Routledge.

Chapter 8
Systemic change always

My escape proves the problem

I need to tell you something uncomfortable: the fact that I escaped doesn't mean the system is fine.

This should be obvious. Apparently it's not.

Because every time someone escapes crushing circumstances through individual effort, people use it as evidence the system works brilliantly and everyone else just needs to try harder.

"See? He made it out. If you just try hard enough, you can too."

Which is bollocks of the highest order.

I escaped because I had specific privileges most people lack—age, pension, property, passport, education, health, neurodivergence that finds change energising.

Remove any of those and I'd still be in Gawler, worrying about hot water systems.

But here's what really bothers me: there's this assumption that individual escape absolves systemic problems.

"Good for you! Now shut up about people still trapped."

Except talking about it does help. Or might. Because individual solutions only work for individuals with required privileges.

Systemic solutions work for everyone.

And I wonder why we're so invested in individual solutions when systemic solutions would actually address problems rather than just helping lucky individuals escape whilst everyone else remains trapped.

Let's talk about resilience

Resilience is possibly my least favourite word in the mental health lexicon, and I say that as someone whose lexicon includes "moist" and "irregardless."

Resilience is what we call it when people survive circumstances that shouldn't exist.

It's a brilliant linguistic trick. Take a failure of social design, rebrand it as opportunity for personal growth, then celebrate people who don't die from it.

Someone's working three jobs and still can't afford rent? Wow, so resilient.

Someone's navigating poverty whilst managing chronic illness with inadequate healthcare? Amazing resilience.

Someone's maintaining employment despite being in abusive relationship because they can't afford to leave? Such resilience.

We've turned survival of hostile circumstances into virtue. Which is deeply convenient for everyone who benefits from those circumstances remaining hostile.

It's like setting up obstacle course designed to injure people, then giving awards to those who make it through whilst acting like the obstacle course is fine.

Maybe we should make obstacles sharper to build even more character?

Resilience is what we demand when we refuse to provide support

Here's what frustrates me: celebrating resilience means we don't have to fix systems requiring people to be resilient.

We can just celebrate individuals who survive whilst quietly ignoring ones who don't.

I've been called resilient more times than I can count.

"You're so resilient! You've overcome so much!"

And I appreciate the sentiment. People mean well.

But every time someone calls me resilient, I think: I shouldn't have had to be.

I shouldn't have needed resilience to survive on military pension in wealthy country. That's not resilience—that's systemic failure with good PR.

I shouldn't have needed resilience to access pension I was entitled to after serving. That's not resilience—that's bureaucratic hostility.

I shouldn't have needed resilience to survive as neurodivergent person in systems designed exclusively for neurotypical brains. That's not resilience—that's discrimination with extra steps.

Calling it resilience reframes systemic problems as individual challenges to overcome through personal strength.

Which sounds empowering until you realise it means systems never have to change.

Psychological contracts and society

Let me tell you about psychological contracts again, because apparently I can't write a book without banging on about research I conducted decades ago.

My research was about organisational psychological contracts—unwritten agreements between employers and employees.

But the same framework applies to social contracts between citizens and societies.

Society promises: if you contribute, you'll be rewarded. If you work hard, you'll have security. If you follow rules, you'll be treated fairly. If you serve your country, you'll be taken care of.

These aren't written contracts. They're implied. Expected. The foundation of why people cooperate with social systems.

When organisations violate psychological contracts, research shows consistent outcomes: decreased trust, reduced commitment, increased stress and depression.

Makes sense. You promised something, didn't deliver, people respond negatively to betrayal.

But when societies violate psychological contracts, we don't call it contract violation.

Thatcher and Reagan called it "personal responsibility."

Revolutionary, no?

You worked hard but you're still poor? Should have worked smarter.

You followed rules but you're still struggling? Should have made better choices.

You served your country but your pension doesn't cover survival? Should have planned better.

The contract violation is reframed as individual failure.

Which is brilliant if your goal is maintaining systems that benefit some enormously whilst crushing others systematically.

Because if it's individual failure, individuals need to change. Need to try harder. Need to be more resilient.

But if it's contract violation, systems need to change.

And changing systems is hard.

What systemic change would actually look like

Here's what systemic change would look like if we were serious about it:

Economic systems that don't create poverty:

Universal basic income ensuring everyone has enough to survive without degrading means-testing or forced compliance with pointless rules.

Not complicated. Give people money. Trust them to use it. Research shows they do—they don't become lazy parasites. They make better decisions.

But that would require acknowledging poverty is systemic rather than individual moral failure, and would cost money currently going to tax breaks for corporations.

Healthcare systems that address circumstances:

What if healthcare assessed circumstances before prescribing medication?

"You're depressed. Let's check: Are you poor? In unsafe housing? Chronically stressed by work? Socially isolated? Right, let's address those circumstances rather than just medicating your reasonable response."

Would require healthcare systems addressing social determinants rather than just treating symptoms. Would require doctors having time to talk to patients. Would require funding for social support.

Would require acknowledging health isn't just about bodies but about circumstances.

Workplace systems for neurological diversity:

What if workplaces assumed human brains come in varieties and designed environments to accommodate diversity by default?

Quiet spaces and collaborative spaces. Flexible hours and predictable schedules. Assessment based on output rather than face time.

None of this is revolutionary. None particularly expensive. Just requires acknowledging neurotypical extroverts aren't only valid type of human.

But that would require employers to stop demanding conformity, and conformity is easier to manage.

Welfare systems that support rather than punish:

What if welfare systems assumed people were telling truth rather than lying?

No means-testing requiring repeatedly proving poverty. No forced compliance with degrading activities. No surveillance treating recipients as suspects. No arbitrary rules trapping people in poverty.

Just: you need support, here's support, we trust you.

Research shows this works better than current hostile approach. But it would require trusting people.

Cultural systems with broader definitions:

What if cultures acknowledged acceptable ways of being human are broader than current narrow definitions?

What if introversion wasn't treated as something to overcome? What if neurodivergent communication styles were accepted? What if men could be emotionally open? What if women could be direct?

What if we just expanded tolerance for human diversity instead of having one acceptable way to be human?

This wouldn't even cost money. Would just require cultural change.

Would require people who fit current definitions accepting their way isn't only acceptable way.

Why don't we do any of this?

Here's the uncomfortable question: why don't we do any of this?

It's not because we don't know these things would work. The research is clear. The evidence is overwhelming. We have proof.

It's because changing systems requires acknowledging current systems benefit some people enormously at expense of others.

Requires wealthy people accepting higher taxes instead of accumulating wealth they couldn't spend in seventeen lifetimes.

Requires employers accommodating diverse neurologies even when it's less convenient.

Requires healthcare systems funding social support rather than profitable pharmaceuticals.

Requires cultural change making currently-comfortable people slightly less comfortable.

And that's hard.

Not impossible—humans have managed harder things. Just hard.

So instead we celebrate resilience and tell individuals to cope better, and act like this is fine.

I benefit from current systems whilst being harmed by them

I need to acknowledge something: I'm writing this from position of comfort that makes advocacy considerably easier.

My circumstances are no longer crushing me. My depression has lifted. My life in Đà Lạt is genuinely pleasant.

That makes it easy to advocate for systemic change.

When you're trapped in crushing circumstances, advocating feels impossible because you're too busy surviving.

So I'm not arguing that trapped people should become activists whilst also surviving. Should organise protests whilst working three jobs.

That's unreasonable.

I'm arguing that people who've escaped—who have privilege and comfort and capacity—have obligation to advocate for systemic change on behalf of people still trapped.

Because if we don't, systems never change.

And individual escape remains only solution, available only to people with sufficient privilege.

I also need to acknowledge: I benefit from current systems even whilst being harmed by them.

I'm white man with education and citizenship in a wealthy country. Former RAAF, which gives me veteran status and respect even though my pension is inadequate.

I have privileges that protected me even when I was poor, that enabled my escape, that mean I'm taken seriously when I write books criticising systems.

If I were woman, or person of colour, or transgender, or visibly disabled—would I have had same opportunities? Would I have same platform?

Probably not.

So I'm arguing for systemic change from position of having benefited from systemic advantages.

Which is awkward but also kind of the point.

Because changing systems would reduce some of my privileges. Would mean paying more taxes. Would mean sharing resources more equitably.

And I'm okay with that.

I'd rather live in society where everyone has enough than one where I have plenty whilst others suffer.

But I recognise that position is easier to take from here in Đà Lạt where my pension covers comfortable living.

Change is possible when three conditions align

Here's what my research on psychological contracts revealed about change:

Change is possible when three conditions align:

First: Recognition that current arrangements aren't working. Not "could be better" but "are actively causing harm."

Second: Belief that different arrangements are possible. Not utopian fantasy but realistic alternatives with evidence.

Third: Will to implement change even when uncomfortable for people who benefit from current arrangements.

We have first two.

Depression rates are skyrocketing—clear evidence current arrangements aren't working.

We have proof systemic changes work—UBI studies, workplace accommodation research, healthcare reform evidence.

What we lack is third: will to change even when uncomfortable.

Because changing systems is uncomfortable. Requires acknowledging current systems are unjust. Requires people with privilege accepting they'd have less privilege in fairer systems. Requires actual sacrifice rather than performative concern.

And it's so much easier to just tell individuals to be more resilient.

Individual solutions AND systemic advocacy

Here's a contrarian thought: maybe individual solutions and systemic advocacy aren't opposed.

Maybe you can change your circumstances whilst acknowledging most people can't.

Maybe you can escape whilst advocating for better systems so escape isn't necessary.

Maybe you can be grateful for privileges whilst working to extend them to everyone.

This isn't either/or. It's both/and.

I changed my circumstances because I could. Because I had privileges that made it possible. Because I got lucky.

And now I'm writing this book arguing systems should change so people don't need my particular privileges to survive.

Some people will see this as hypocrisy. "You benefited from the system and now you're criticising it?"

Yes. Exactly.

Because benefitting from unjust systems doesn't mean you have to defend them. You can benefit from something whilst recognising it's unjust and advocating for change.

In fact, you probably should, because you're better positioned to advocate if you're not actively being crushed.

Both things can be true simultaneously.

Both things need to be true simultaneously.

The veteran example

Let me tell you about veterans again, because they're perfect example of why systemic change matters.

Australian veterans are told: be resilient. Overcome trauma through personal strength. Adapt to civilian life. Don't be burden. Get on with it.

Individual solutions offered: therapy, medication, support groups, resilience training, ceremonies thanking you for service whilst providing nothing material.

All potentially helpful. All treating symptoms whilst leaving systemic problems intact.

Meanwhile, systemic problems creating veteran depression remain unchanged:

Pensions below poverty line after you factor in the considerable costs of medicines and medical/psychiatric help. Healthcare requiring exhausting navigation of deliberately obtuse bureaucracy. Housing assistance inadequate or non-existent. Employment support minimal. Transition programs chronically underfunded.

And fundamental betrayal underlying it all: serve your country, get abandoned afterwards, get told you should be more resilient about abandonment.

You can't resilience your way out of systemic betrayal.

You can't therapy away poverty caused by inadequate pensions.

You can't medicate through bureaucratic hostility.

You can survive circumstances that would otherwise kill you. Which is admirable but shouldn't be necessary.

The solution isn't making veterans more resilient. It's designing systems that don't betray people who serve.

Adequate pensions. Accessible healthcare. Housing support that's actually supportive. Employment assistance that works. Actual care rather than performative thanking.

This would cost money. Would require political will. Would mean acknowledging we're abandoning veterans whilst pretending to honour them.

Much easier to just call them resilient and stand at the top of our driveways one dawn per year, and sell poppies.

What if we stopped treating systemic change as impossible?

Here's what I wonder: what if we stopped treating systemic change as impossible and started treating it as difficult?

Impossible means: can't be done, no point trying, might as well focus on individual solutions.

Difficult means: hard, requires effort and sacrifice and political will, but possible if we commit.

We have evidence systemic changes work.

UBI studies show positive results. Workplace accommodation research shows benefits. Healthcare reform in other countries shows better outcomes. Welfare redesigns show trust works better than surveillance.

It's not impossible. It's just difficult.

And we've convinced ourselves difficult equals impossible so we don't have to try.

But what if we tried?

What if we implemented UBI and discovered it reduced depression at scale?

What if we redesigned workplaces for neurological diversity and discovered productivity improved?

What if we trusted welfare recipients and discovered fraud rates were minimal whilst wellbeing improved?

What if we funded healthcare addressing social determinants and discovered it cost less than endless pharmaceutical interventions?

We won't know unless we try.

And we won't try as long as we're invested in believing systems can't change, only individuals can.

Both/and, not either/or

Here's my bottom line:

Individual change when possible. Systemic change always.

Not individual change instead of systemic change.

Not systemic change instead of individual change.

Both. Simultaneously. Continuously. Messily.

Change your circumstances if you can. Escape if possible. Do whatever you need to survive and possibly flourish.

And also: advocate for systemic change so fewer people need to escape because systems work better for more people.

This isn't either/or. It's both/and.

Maybe if enough people who've escaped continue advocating instead of pulling ladder up, eventually we'll reach critical mass required to actually change systems.

I don't know if that's possible.

Humans have remarkable capacity for maintaining comfortable injustice whilst performing concern.

But I wonder if it might be possible.

If enough people decided fairer systems were worth discomfort of change. If enough people with privilege decided to use it for advocacy. If enough people recognised we're all better off when everyone's okay.

And wondering is where change starts—with questioning whether things that seem impossible might just be difficult, and whether difficult things are worth attempting even when we're not certain they'll work.

I think they are.

But I'm a contrarian, so what do I know?

Hope without guarantees

I want to be clear about something: I'm not offering certainty about whether systemic change will happen.

I'm not offering solutions that will definitely work.

I'm not offering toxic positivity disguised as hope.

What I'm offering is evidence that systems can change because they've changed before. That we know what works because research exists.

That individual transformations suggest systemic transformations are possible.

And also: my own stubborn insistence that we should try even if we're not certain it'll work.

Because trying is better than accepting crushing circumstances as inevitable whilst telling people to be more resilient.

Individual escape is valid. Take it if you can.

But don't stop advocating for systemic change just because you're no longer being crushed.

Because if everyone who escapes stops caring about people still trapped, systems perpetuate themselves indefinitely.

And I'd rather try and fail than not try because I'm comfortable now.

So that's it, then. Individual change when possible. Systemic advocacy always. Both/and, not either/or.

Change what you can. Advocate for changing what you can't change alone. Trust your experience. Question everything. Maintain cosmic perspective.

Simple, right?

Except there's one more thing I need to address. One more question that's been lurking throughout this entire book, implicit in every chapter but never directly confronted.

Hope.

Is it helpful? Is it necessary? Is it honest?

Or is "hope" just another thing we celebrate whilst not addressing circumstances that make people hopeless?

I spent most of my life without hope, and I survived. I have something resembling hope now, tentatively, uncertainly, and I'm not entirely sure what to do with it or whether it matters.

Because here's what I keep coming back to: my depression didn't lift because I became more hopeful. It lifted because my circumstances changed materially in ways that made hope possible again.

Hope didn't create change. Change created hope.

So maybe the question isn't "how do we give people hope?" Maybe it's "how do we create circumstances where hope emerges naturally rather than requiring constant effort to maintain?"

Maybe it's "how do we build systems that don't require people to be hopeful about surviving them?"

Let me tell you about hope without toxicity. About cosmic perspective and uncertain futures and why I'm cautiously optimistic despite everything whilst also questioning whether optimism itself is the right framework.

One last chapter. One last wondering about what might be possible if we actually tried.

References

Friedli, L., & Stearn, R. (2015). Positive affect as coercive strategy: Conditionality, activation and the role of psychology in UK government workfare programmes. *Medical Humanities, 41*(1), 40-47.

Marmot, M. (2015). *The health gap: The challenge of an unequal world.* London: Bloomsbury.

Mills, C. W. (1959). *The sociological imagination.* Oxford University Press.

Robinson, S. L., & Rousseau, D. M. (1994). Violating the psychological contract: Not the exception but the norm. *Journal of Organizational Behavior, 15*(3), 245-259.

Wilkinson, R., & Pickett, K. (2009). *The spirit level: Why greater equality makes societies stronger.* New York: Bloomsbury Press.

Chapter 9
Hope without toxicity

Cautiously optimistic about the future

I need to tell you something that might seem contradictory after eight chapters arguing depression is often reasonable response to unreasonable circumstances: I'm cautiously optimistic about the future.

Not in toxic positivity way involving gratitude journals and manifesting abundance and possibly crystals arranged in sacred geometry.

Not in denial-of-reality way pretending everything's fine when it demonstrably isn't.

But in a "humans have managed harder things than fixing crushing systems, so maybe we could try that" sort of way.

Which isn't the most inspiring rallying cry. But I'm a psychologist, not a motivational speaker.

And I don't believe in lying to make people feel better temporarily whilst leaving circumstances unchanged.

What I mean by hope without toxicity

Let me be clear about what I mean, because the difference matters enormously.

Toxic hope says: Think positively and everything will work out. Your attitude determines reality. If you're still struggling, you're not hoping hard enough. Manifest better.

It's victim-blaming dressed as empowerment.

Toxic hope denies reality. Pretends circumstances don't matter. Blames individuals for systemic problems by suggesting they could think their way out.

It's resilience mythology wearing a smiley face mask.

Non-toxic hope—the kind I'm cautiously endorsing despite instinctive suspicion—acknowledges reality whilst believing change is possible.

It says: These circumstances are genuinely difficult. Your response is reasonable. The systems are unjust. And also—separately, additionally, not instead of—things could be different if we collectively decided to make them different.

Not through individual mindset shifts but through actual material changes to actual circumstances.

That's the hope I'm talking about.

The kind grounded in evidence that systemic changes work, combined with uncertainty about whether we'll actually implement them, combined with stubborn insistence we should try even if we're not certain it'll work.

I spent most of my life without hope

I spent most of my life without hope, which sounds dramatically depressing but was actually just realistic assessment. I made Robert Smith sound like the aural equivalent of sunshine.

When you're poor and depressed and neurodivergent in systems designed for wealthy neurotypical people, hope feels like luxury you can't afford.

Every time I tried to hope—tried to believe things would get better, circumstances would improve, promises would be honoured—life demonstrated hope was foolish and possibly dangerous.

Business ventures failed despite enormous effort. Financial crises erupted despite careful planning. Depression persisted despite trying everything.

So I stopped hoping.

Not in dramatic giving-up way but in quiet protecting-myself way. Like pulling in your arms when walking through narrow space so you don't get hurt.

And here's what's interesting: stopping hoping didn't make me less depressed.

It just made me depressed without additional burden of disappointed hope.

Which was marginally better but not actually helpful because circumstances remained unchanged.

What actually helped was changing circumstances, not changing hope.

Vietnam didn't work because I hoped it would. It worked because material conditions improved.

Same brain. Same capacity for hope or lack thereof. Completely different circumstances producing completely different outcomes.

But here's the thing that bothers me: I'm now experiencing something resembling hope, and I'm not entirely certain what to do with it.

What gives me hope

Let me tell you what gives me hope—actual hope, not toxic positivity.

First: We have proof systemic changes work.

Not theories. Actual evidence from actual studies.

UBI experiments show consistent results: people don't become lazy, they make better decisions, mental health improves, depression decreases. Finland, Kenya, Canada, India—different cultures, same results.

Workplace accommodation research shows designing for neurological diversity benefits everyone.

Healthcare systems addressing social determinants produce better outcomes for less money.

Welfare systems trusting recipients produce better outcomes whilst costing less.

This isn't wishful thinking. This is data. Proof that different approaches work better.

We know what works. We just haven't decided to implement it at scale.

But the knowledge exists. The evidence is there.

That's hope grounded in evidence.

Second: Systems have changed before.

This should be obvious. Apparently isn't.

People act like current systems are natural laws rather than human constructions that could be reconstructed differently.

Slavery was a system. Then it wasn't, in most places, eventually, after enormous struggle.

Women couldn't vote or own property. Then they could, after enormous struggle.

LGBTQ+ people were criminalised, pathologised, killed. Then, in some places, they could marry and exist openly, after enormous struggle.

Systems change. Not easily. Not without enormous effort and sacrifice.

But they change.

And changes that seemed impossible before they happened are now taken for granted as obvious moral progress.

Which suggests current systems that seem unchangeable might also be changeable if enough people decided they were unjust and worth changing.

That's hope grounded in historical evidence.

Third: Individual transformations suggest systemic transformations are possible.

I'm evidence of this, though I recognise the irony of using my individual transformation as evidence for systemic possibilities.

But here's what my transformation demonstrates: brains don't have to be fixed when environments can be changed.

I'm same person with same neurology with same history with same everything except circumstances, and depression that persisted for decades lifted when circumstances changed.

Not because I tried harder. Not because I manifested abundance. Not because I finally had the right attitude.

Because circumstances changed materially in ways that supported my neurology instead of crushing it.

If that's possible for individuals—if same brain can produce completely different outcomes in different environments—then it's possible for societies.

We could design environments supporting human flourishing. Could create economic systems not requiring poverty. Could build workplaces accommodating neurological diversity. Could implement welfare systems that support rather than punish.

My transformation doesn't prove the Australian system is fine. It proves systems matter enormously and different systems produce different outcomes.

That's hope based on lived experience.

Fourth: The fact that so many people are depressed suggests systems are the problem.

If depression rates are skyrocketing despite increasing access to medication and therapy and wellness programs—what does that tell you?

Either:

A) Human brains are increasingly defective through unknown mechanisms, or

B) Systems are increasingly hostile to human flourishing and depression is reasonable response.

I'm going with B.

Which means solution isn't fixing millions of individual brains. It's fixing systems crushing them.

And that's actually hopeful in a strange way, because fixing systems is theoretically possible even if politically difficult.

If problem is systemic, systemic solutions exist. We just have to implement them.

I don't know if hope is helpful

Let me be honest about something: I don't know if hope is helpful.

I spent decades without it and survived. I have it now, tentatively, and it makes things more pleasant but I'm not certain it's necessary.

Maybe hope is another thing we celebrate because it sounds nice whilst not actually addressing circumstances that make people hopeless.

Maybe we should stop demanding people be hopeful about genuinely hopeless circumstances and instead change circumstances so people don't need hope to survive them.

Maybe hope is what we offer when we don't want to offer material support. Like thoughts and prayers after preventable tragedies—sounds compassionate, costs nothing, changes nothing.

I don't know.

What I know: whether or not hope is helpful, circumstances matter enormously, and changing circumstances produces different outcomes regardless of hope levels.

My depression lifted when circumstances changed, not when hope changed.

Veterans suffer because circumstances are crushing them, not because they lack hope.

People struggle in poverty because poverty is materially difficult, not because they're insufficiently hopeful.

So maybe the question isn't "how do we give people hope?" but "how do we change circumstances so people don't need hope to survive them?"

Maybe we stop celebrating hope and start implementing changes.

What genuine hope looks like

Here's what I think genuine hope looks like, lying awake at 2am in Đà Lạt:

It looks like acknowledging reality whilst believing different realities are possible.

It looks like validating suffering whilst working to eliminate causes rather than just helping individuals cope better.

It looks like individual change when possible combined with systemic advocacy always. Not instead of. Both/and continuously messily.

It looks like questioning whether hope itself is right framework whilst maintaining it anyway because alternative is accepting crushing circumstances as inevitable.

It looks like trusting humans can design better systems if we decide to, whilst acknowledging we might not decide to because comfortable people rarely volunteer for discomfort.

It looks like uncertainty about everything except certainty that current systems are unjust and could be different and we should try even if we're not certain it'll work.

Not inspiring in motivational poster way.

But honest in way toxic positivity never is.

Photography one last time

I want to tell you about photography one final time, because it's been my evidence throughout and illustrates something about hope.

When I was in Adelaide, I photographed in black and white. Not because I preferred it aesthetically—though I told myself that—but because colour felt like lying.

Colour suggested vibrancy and life and possibility. None of those felt true.

Black and white felt honest. Stark. Real. Classic. Fine Art.

I didn't decide this consciously. Wasn't making artistic statements. Just documented what I saw, and what I saw was grey.

In Vietnam, colour returned to my photography before I consciously recognised it was returning to my life.

I'd photograph markets and notice images had colour. Would edit them and not immediately strip it out. Would look at results and think: this is okay. This isn't lying.

Colour wasn't choice. It was acknowledgment that circumstances had changed enough that vibrancy felt true rather than false.

That's what hope looks like in practice: not deciding to be hopeful or choosing optimism, but circumstances changing enough that hope emerges naturally.

You can't photograph your way into hope any more than you can think your way out of depression.

But you can document what's actually there, and sometimes what's actually there changes, and that tells you something about how profoundly circumstances affect perception.

I look at my photography now—vibrant colour, people smiling, light that looks warm—and think: is this evidence of recovery or just evidence of better circumstances?

Probably both.

Definitely something that wouldn't have happened if circumstances hadn't changed materially.

What I'm not offering

Let me tell you what I'm not offering in this final chapter:

I'm not offering certainty. Not about recovery, not about future, not about whether systemic change will happen or Vietnam will continue working or depression will stay away.

Life doesn't offer certainty. The universe is fundamentally uncertain and pretending otherwise is comforting but false.

I'm not offering solutions. Not "do these five things and your depression will lift" or "implement these policies and everyone will flourish." I have no 12-step program to sell you.

I'm offering observations about what worked for me whilst acknowledging it might not work for you, combined with evidence about systemic changes that work at scale whilst acknowledging implementing them is politically difficult.

Messy. Uncertain. Imperfect. Honest.

I'm not offering toxic positivity. Not "everything happens for a reason" or "just stay positive" or "manifest abundance."

If you're depressed because circumstances are crushing you—and they might be, probably are—that's reasonable. Your response is sane. The circumstances are insane.

I'm not offering false hope that individual solutions will address systemic problems. My escape doesn't mean system is fine. Individual solutions only work for individuals whilst systemic problems continue crushing everyone else.

Both/and, remember?

What I am offering

What I am offering—tentatively, uncertainly, with appropriate caveats:

Evidence that circumstances matter more than mindset. That systems can be changed because they've changed before. That depression often lifts when circumstances change even without individual interventions. That different approaches work better than current approaches. That we know what works and just haven't implemented it yet.

And also: my own confused uncertain imperfect experience of escaping crushing circumstances through privilege and luck, combined with stubborn insistence others shouldn't need my particular privileges to survive.

Not inspirational in conventional way.

But real in way that might be more useful than inspiration.

The bottom line

Here's my bottom line:

Change your circumstances if you can. Escape if possible and you have required privileges. Don't feel guilty about escaping just because others can't.

And also: advocate for systemic change regardless of whether you've escaped or are still trapped. Advocate more urgently if you've escaped because you have capacity trapped people lack.

Trust that reasonable responses to unreasonable circumstances don't require medication unless they do, in which case take medication without shame whilst also questioning why so many people need medication for reasonable responses to systemic problems.

Question everything, including hope itself, including this book, including my recovery and whether it's real or temporary.

Maintain cosmic perspective that we're having this conversation on small planet orbiting an ordinary star in unremarkable galaxy. Which doesn't minimise suffering but provides context allowing for both seriousness about real problems and lightness about our tendency to catastrophise.

And maybe—possibly, tentatively, with appropriate scepticism—believe that humans could design better systems if we decided to.

Cautious optimism grounded in evidence and uncertainty.

Not toxic positivity. Not false hope.

Just: things could be different. We know what works. We could implement it if we wanted to.

Whether we will remains uncertain.

But we could.

The 3am meditation

I'm lying awake at 3am in Đà Lạt, which is better than lying awake at 3am in Gawler but still involves lying awake at 3am.

And I'm thinking about this book, nearly finished, and what I want readers to take from it.

I think I want you to know this: your response to crushing circumstances is probably reasonable even if everyone's telling you it's not.

Your depression might be sane whilst your circumstances are insane.

Your struggles might reflect systemic problems rather than personal failures.

Your difficulties surviving in systems designed for different brains or circumstances or privileges aren't evidence you're broken—they're evidence systems are badly designed.

And also: circumstances can change. Mine did, through privilege and luck and stubbornness and probably other factors I don't understand.

And also: systems could change. Should change. We know how to change them better. Whether we will remains uncertain but possibility exists.

And also: both/and rather than either/or. Individual change when possible and systemic advocacy always.

And also: question everything, including hope itself, including whether anything I've written is true or useful or just one person's rambling, confused experience.

And finally: the universe spent billions of years evolving consciousness. The least we can do is use it thoughtfully rather than turning it into optimisation project or medicating it into submission when it responds reasonably to unreasonable circumstances.

The cosmic frame returns

We're on a small planet orbiting an ordinary star in an unremarkable galaxy.

One of billions of galaxies in a universe so large we can't properly comprehend it.

We're here for a cosmically insignificant amount of time—roughly eighty years if we're lucky, which is less than a blink in cosmic terms.

And during that blink, we've decided to spend enormous energy maintaining systems that make millions of people miserable whilst telling them the problem is their brains rather than our systems.

Which is, when you think about it from cosmic perspective, rather absurd.

Not "ha-ha" absurd. More "what the fuck are we doing?" absurd.

We could be designing systems that support human flourishing. We could be creating environments where people thrive. We could be building societies where everyone has enough.

Instead we're celebrating resilience and medicating reasonable responses to unreasonable circumstances and acting like this is fine.

The universe gave us consciousness. Big brains. Ability to reason and plan and cooperate on massive scales.

And we're using those brains to maintain crushing systems whilst blaming crushed people for not being sufficiently uncrushed.

From cosmic perspective, that's not just tragic. It's embarrassingly stupid.

We can do better.

We have evidence we can do better.

The question is whether we will.

The invitation

So here's to cautious optimism grounded in evidence and uncertainty.

To circumstances that support flourishing rather than crush it.

To systems designed for humans as they actually are rather than narrow definitions of acceptable humanity.

To both/and rather than either/or.

To questions rather than answers.

To wondering what might be possible if we tried.

And to hope—genuine hope, non-toxic hope, hope grounded in evidence rather than wishful thinking, hope acknowledging reality whilst believing different realities are possible.

Cautious. Uncertain. Imperfect.

Real.

I don't know if that's enough.

But it's what I have to offer after sixty-six years living through crushing circumstances, escaping through privilege, and spending too much time thinking about why some people flourish whilst others suffer when possibly it's just circumstances and systems and design choices we've made and could unmake.

Your brain probably isn't broken.

The circumstances might be.

And circumstances can change—individually when possible, systemically always.

Trust your experience. Change what you can. Advocate for what you can't change alone.

And maintain cosmic perspective that we're all just humans on a small planet trying to figure out how to exist together without crushing each other unnecessarily.

Which should be easier than we've made it.

References

Calhoun, L. G., & Tedeschi, R. G. (2006). The foundations of posttraumatic growth: An expanded framework. In L. G. Calhoun & R. G. Tedeschi (Eds.), *Handbook of posttraumatic growth: Research and practice* (pp. 1-23). Lawrence Erlbaum Associates.

Ehrenreich, B. (2009). *Bright-sided: How positive thinking is undermining America*. Metropolitan Books.

Held, B. S. (2004). The negative side of positive psychology. *Journal of Humanistic Psychology, 44*(1), 9-46.

Norem, J. K., & Chang, E. C. (2002). The positive psychology of negative thinking. *Journal of Clinical Psychology, 58*(9), 993-1001.

Snyder, C. R. (2002). Hope theory: Rainbows in the mind. *Psychological Inquiry, 13*(4), 249-275.

Wilkinson, R., & Pickett, K. (2018). *The inner level: How more equal societies reduce stress, restore sanity and improve everyone's well-being*. Allen Lane.

END

About the Author

Lee Hopkins is a counselling psychologist, organisational researcher, and accidental expatriate now living in Đà Lạt, Vietnam. He holds a BSc. (Hons.) in applied psychology and sociology, a master's degree in counselling practice and has over 450 academic mentions for his research on psychological contracts in organizations—which turns out to be surprisingly relevant to understanding why societies betray the people who contribute to them.

He spent decades working with veterans experiencing depression and bipolar disorder, all whilst managing his own depression that persisted despite trying every intervention psychology had to offer. It eventually lifted not through better therapy or increased medication, but through geographic relocation and material change in circumstances—which raised uncomfortable questions about what we're actually treating when we treat depression.

A former Royal Australian Air Force serviceman, Lee survived military service, multiple business failures, financial poverty, and years of navigating Australian bureaucratic systems designed to exhaust people into giving up. He was diagnosed with AuDHD (autism and ADHD) at sixty-six, which explained decades of exhausting masking and why systems designed for neurotypical brains felt like trying to breathe underwater.

His photography has evolved from moody, melancholic black-and-white landscapes to vibrant colour portraits, which he considers the most compelling evidence that environments shape perception more than we'd like to admit.

He writes about systemic problems with the irreverence of someone who's survived them, the rigour of someone who's researched them, and the cosmic humour of someone who recognizes we're all having this conversation on a small planet orbiting an ordinary star, which doesn't minimize suffering but provides useful perspective about our tendency to overcomplicate solutions.

This is not his first book. He's almost certain there will be more, but he's learned not to make predictions about the future because the universe has a dark sense of humour about such things.

~

quiethalf.substack.com :: mindblownpsychology.com

Also by Lee Hopkins

Books

You're not imagining it: It IS this weird

Understanding AuDHD: A comprehensive guide

Embracing neurodiversity: Understanding and thriving with your unique brain

Living with Bipolar II: Understanding, managing, thriving

Rational Suicide: Beyond despair—a reasoned farewell?

Loving across time: Understanding age-gap relationships in the modern world

Love, silence, and VietnamCupid: Tình yêu, sự im lặng, và VietnamCupid

Love in Foreign Languages: A neurodivergent heart's search for cultural compatibility across nine countries

How to be your Possible Self

www.ingramcontent.com/pod-product-compliance
Lightning Source LLC
LaVergne TN
LVHW100320210926
848480LV00003B/1191